THE EAGLE'S SHADOW

THE

EAGLE'S SHADOW

Why America Fascinates and

Infuriates the World

MARK HERTSGAARD

Farrar, Straus and Giroux / New York

Farrar, Straus and Giroux
19 Union Square West, New York 10003

Distributed in Canada by Douglas & McIntyre Ltd.
Printed in the United States of America
First edition, 2002

Library of Congress Cataloging-in-Publication Data
Hertsgaard, Mark, 1956–
    The eagle's shadow : why America fascinates and infuriates the
world / Mark Hertsgaard.
        p. cm.
    Includes index.
    ISBN 0-374-10383-6 (hc : alk. paper)
      1. United States—Foreign public opinion.   I. Title.
E840.2 .H47 2002
973—dc21

                                        2002072231

Designed by Jonathan D. Lippincott

www.fsgbooks.com

1   3   5   7   9   10   8   6   4   2

FOR FRANCESCA

CONTENTS

THE EAGLE'S SHADOW

(1)
THE PAROCHIAL
SUPERPOWER

For Malcolm Adams, as for most people around the world, America is more a mental image than a real place. He will almost certainly never see the United States with his own eyes—he'll never have enough money to afford the trip—but that diminishes his interest in the place not one bit.

I met Malcolm on a bus ride in South Africa in June of 2001. He was a driver for the Baz Bus, a shuttle service known to the backpacker crowd in South Africa as a cheap if not always reliable way to get between major cities and rural tourist areas. The day he picked me up, he was heading east along the coast toward Durban. It was late afternoon, a low winter sun. Along the roadside hundreds of people, bunched in groups of five or six, were walking home. Off to our right, the Indian Ocean frothed and sparkled, crashing against the southern edge of the African landmass.

Malcolm was thirty-two, but his smooth-skinned face and ebullient demeanor made him look younger. Like his father, he had worked as a driver all his adult life, though as a teenager he dreamed of becoming a naval officer. "I had the ability," he explained wistfully, "but under the old system your skin color could keep you out of those things." Now he worked fourteen-hour days driving from one end of South Africa to the other. The scenery was glorious, but he missed his wife and two children, whom he saw only on weekends.

Still, he said, this was an improvement over his last job, driving public buses for the city of Cape Town. He quit that job after five fellow drivers were murdered gangland-style while driving their routes. The killer later testified in court that for each murder he was paid 350 rand, about U.S. $50, by bosses of the taxi drivers union, who apparently hoped to frighten passengers into taxis.

"Yeah, I heard about those shootings," I said. "The newspapers back home wrote about them."

"And where is back home?" Malcolm asked.

I told him, and his eyes lit up with glee as he gushed, "Oh, you are from America! Your country has a very great influence on South Africa."

"Really?" I said. "Good or bad?"

"Good, good! America is what everyone here wants to be like—American music, American clothes, American lifestyle: nice house, big car, lots of cash. America is the idol for many people in South Africa."

His own clothes made the point: a Jack Daniel's baseball cap, black jeans, and a royal blue ski jacket with puffy sleeves. He would have fit right in on the streets of Brooklyn or St. Louis. Malcolm said he and his friends knew about America from songs they heard on the radio, movies they rented at the video shop, TV shows carried on South African channels; *The Bold and the Beautiful* was a particular favorite. I asked whether older people shared his view—did his mother and father idolize the United States? "No, they are more Christian,"

4

he replied without irony. "They want to live a South African life."

By now, darkness had fallen. Malcolm's face glowed in the reflection of the dashboard lights as he spoke of the Cape Town township where he and his family lived. They had running water, electric light, and paved streets, but many neighbors lacked real jobs and crime was a constant worry: "Gangsters are shooting and robbing people and the police do nothing." We were silent a moment. Then, with the same enthusiasm he showed for anything American, he added, "Did you know that every township in South Africa has two street gangs named for your country?"

"No."

"Yes! One is called the Young Americans, the other is called the Ugly Americans."

"What's the difference?"

A wide smile. "The Young Americans dress like Americans. The Ugly Americans shoot like Americans."

GOOD, BAD, BUT NEVER INDIFFERENT

America: a place that is very rich and shoots lots of guns. It's not the most sophisticated analysis, but it's a fair shorthand for how the United States is seen by many people around the world. Friend or foe, rich or poor, foreigners tend to fear America for its awesome military power even as they are dazzled by its shimmering wealth.

That perspective may sound jarring to some Americans. We see ourselves as decent, hardworking people who wish the rest of the world well and do more than our share to help it. We are proud of our freedom and prosperous way of life, and we understand why others want the same. We would rather not "entangle our peace and prosperity" in foreign toils, as the father of our country, George Washington, advised long ago, but we will use force if necessary to oppose injustice and protect freedom around the world for ourselves and others. We have our shortcomings like anyone else, but we believe we live in the greatest country in the world.

Malcolm Adams would, I imagine, agree with that assessment, and he's not alone. In twenty years of living and traveling overseas through thirty countries, I have spoken with many people who think very highly of America and Americans. I have also, of course, met many who find fault with the United States. In fact, the same individual often fits in both categories; some of the most penetrating criticisms of America I've heard came from people who, by and large, admire the place.

I began working on this book long before the 2001 terror attacks against America, and I pursued my travels and interviews both before and after September 11. From the start, the book was intended for two separate but related audiences. I hoped to provide my fellow Americans with a sort of traveler's report: "This is how we look to the rest of the world." For non-American readers, I hoped to explain why America and Americans are the way we are. The September 11 attacks gave these goals greater urgency and focus by suddenly illuminating how people everywhere felt about the United States. But the attacks also complicated the project by leaving Americans understandably sensitive to anything approaching candid criticism of their country.

A year has now passed since the terrible explosions and fires that killed more than three thousand people in New York, Washington, and Pennsylvania—a year of healing, of taking stock, of fighting back. Are Americans at last ready to hear what people overseas think about us? The message is a lot more complex than the "Why They Hate Us" war cry our media have supplied. And a lot more interesting. Foreigners aren't always right about America, far from it. But neither are they merely embittered fanatics, or jealous of our money, or resentful of our power, or animated by any of the other stock explanations mainstream American pundits and politicians have advanced as substitutes for honest self-examination. Most foreigners are sophisticated enough to see both the good and the bad about the United States, the pluses and the minuses. Which is why Americans can learn from their perceptions, if we choose to.

Foreigners can see things about America that natives cannot, and if ever there was a time when Americans needed such perspective, it's now. The horror of what happened on September 11 commands us to look at our homeland with new eyes—in particular, with the eyes of the rest of the world. Osama bin Laden and the Taliban are not representative of international opinion; hatred of America, though intense where it exists, is relatively rare. But Americans should not take false comfort from that, or let the sense of victimhood tragically earned on September 11 blind us to the fact that on September 10 the rest of the world harbored plenty of complaints against us, often with good reason. Indeed, some of the tartest criticisms—of the Bush administration's withdrawal from both the Kyoto protocol on global warming and the Anti-Ballistic Missile Treaty, and of the refusal of the United States to join the international criminal court—were coming from the very leaders who soon stood shoulder to shoulder with America against terrorism, notably British prime minister Tony Blair, German chancellor Gerhard Schröder, and French president Jacques Chirac.

To foreigners, there is no contradiction between criticizing the United States one minute and praising it the next. In fact, America's dialectical qualities are part of what makes it so fascinating. The journey around the world I made for this book began in May 2001, ended in November, and included stops in fifteen countries in Europe, the Middle East, Africa, and Asia. During these and previous travels, I've been fortunate to gather opinions about the United States from a wide range of sources: sophisticated business and political leaders, starry-eyed teenagers, multilingual intellectuals, illiterate peasants, workers, housewives, journalists, and more than a few would-be immigrants. Time after time I've been struck by how elites and ordinary folk alike feel both admiring and uneasy about America, envious and appalled, enchanted but dismissive. It is this complex catalogue of impressions—good, bad, but never indifferent—that Americans must confront if we are to transcend the tragedy of September 11 and understand our place in the twenty-first-century world.

"YOU KNOW NOTHING ABOUT US"

The first time I traveled around the world, starting in 1991, I was investigating the environmental future for my book *Earth Odyssey*. Most people in the nineteen countries I visited were happy enough to answer my ecological questions, but often their comments were more dutiful than animated. America, by contrast, is a subject that never fails to get people talking. Everyone has an opinion about it, and they aren't shy about expressing it. Compare, for example, the wide-eyed admiration of Malcolm Adams with the views of three retired terrorists I interviewed a few weeks earlier in a dusty tea shop in

Cairo's Islamic Quarter (even terrorists, it seems, eventually retire). For these graybeards with ankle-length gowns and bubbling water pipes, America was a contemptible bully—a protector of Israel and corrupter of Egypt's Arabic soul. Yet even they had fond memories of Hollywood movies starring Kirk Douglas and Anthony Quinn.

One way or another, foreigners can hardly avoid forming opinions about the United States. Wherever they look, America is in their face. American movies, television, music, fashion, and food have especially captivated young people throughout the world even as they spread America's most important export: its consumer lifestyle and the individualism it promotes. The Internet, computers, and high-tech gadgets revolutionizing daily life all over the planet either originated in the United States or find their fullest development there. America's nuclear arsenal has held life-and-death power over humanity since the bombings of Hiroshima and Nagasaki in 1945. For even longer, the United States economy has been the world's main engine of growth and innovation, and it remains today the "buyer of last resort" whose imports spell the difference between recession and prosperity for rich and poor nations alike.

To top it all off, America receives a disproportionate amount of coverage from news media around the world, reinforcing foreigners' sense of living always in the Eagle's shadow. "I'm glad I live in South Africa and not in the United States," a young white restaurant manager in Stellenbosch, the wine-growing region east of Cape Town, told me. "Any stupid thing that happens in the States is news all over the world: O. J. Simpson, the Florida election recount." Did he resent America's ubiquity? "It's not a matter of resentment," he replied. "It's just fact. I have to listen to what [U.S. Federal

Reserve chairman] Alan Greenspan says. It can affect my inventory. Actually, I think we have an advantage over you, because we know everything about you and you know nothing about us."

Good point. But I would go further: Americans not only don't know much about the rest of the world, we don't care. Or at least we didn't before the terrible events of September 11, 2001. Until then, many Americans were barely aware the outside world existed, a fact that both exasperates and amuses foreigners.

"I went to Tennessee a few years ago to attend my sister's wedding to an American guy," Luis, a musician in Seville, Spain, told me. "When people heard my accent, they asked where I was from. I said Spain. They smiled, Americans are friendly people, and they asked, 'Is that in Mexico?' They were not joking." Even high-powered Americans sometimes know little about the world beyond. Who can forget former president Ronald Reagan's imperishable comment after his first visit to South America? "You'd be surprised," he told reporters, "they're all individual countries down there." True, Reagan's two immediate successors, George Bush and Bill Clinton, were worldly men, but George W. Bush had traveled abroad only three times before he became president. Whatever his other qualities as a leader, in this respect the younger Bush was perfectly representative of his fellow citizens, only 14 percent of whom have passports.

This is the first of many inequalities that distort America's relationship with the rest of the world: foreigners have to care about America, while Americans have traditionally cared little if at all about them. A corollary is that Americans have no idea how they appear to others; the privileged rarely do. After the September 11 attacks, 52 percent of American opinion leaders surveyed by the Pew Research Center for the People and the Press modestly agreed that "America does a lot of good in the world." Only 21 percent of their overseas counterparts shared that sunny assessment of the United States.

There are understandable reasons for Americans' lack of interest in the outside world, starting with geography. Because the United States is so immense and protected on two sides by oceans, the rest of the world seems very far away. Americans lack the sense, so common on other continents, that foreign peoples with different languages, cultures, and beliefs live just over the next ridge or river. (Yes, the United States shares borders with Mexico and Canada, but many U.S. citizens regard their neighbors as honorary junior Americans, welcome as long as they stay in their place.) America's mind-boggling abundance also helps encourage a complacent isolationism. Why bother with the rest of the world when, as a Linda Ronstadt song declares, "everything you want, we got it right here in the U.S.A."?

Nevertheless, I have long felt baffled and disappointed by my countrymen and countrywomen's lack of curiosity about the world. Baffled because I myself find the rest of the world so fascinating, disappointed because I think ignorance of our neighbors reflects badly on Americans. Traveling twice around the world has taught me that Americans have no monopoly on parochialism and self-centeredness; the difference is, Americans are parochial and self-centered at the same time that we are the mightiest power in history. What our political, military, economic, cultural, and scientific institutions do has a decisive influence on the lives of people everywhere on earth, shaping the answers to such questions as "Will I have a job next month?" and "Will there be war?" right down to "What's on television tonight?" But with power comes responsibility.

Americans' indifference to the world bothers me, I guess, because it seems wrong to have so much power over others and not care more about how it gets exercised.

Wrong and, after September 11, also foolish. If Americans rarely paid much attention to the outside world in the past, it's because we thought we didn't have to. As the richest, most powerful nation in history, the United States could do what it wanted, when it wanted. If foreigners didn't like it, so what?

That invincible image never matched reality, of course. Remember Vietnam? And the gasoline lines after the OPEC oil embargo in the 1970s? And the Iranian hostage crisis? But alas, many Americans don't remember. As a people forever fixated on the promise of a better tomorrow, Americans are barely familiar with our history, much less anyone else's. Besides, any unhappy memories were erased by the reassertion of American power directed during the 1980s by Ronald Reagan, a man who, despite his Alzheimer's disease, remains to this day America's most powerful politician (a theme elaborated later in this book). In the eyes of many Americans, the fall of the Berlin Wall in 1989 was proof that the United States was the chosen nation of God, as Reagan and other Cold Warriors had long proclaimed. And then came the roaring 1990s, when the United States experienced an explosion of economic growth that rewarded the wealthy out of all proportion while—brilliant touch—appearing accessible to anyone with the wit to trade stocks over the Internet. As the Dow and Nasdaq exchanges soared ever higher, creating countless new millionaires every day, who cared what was going on in the rest of the world? Clearly, America was where the action was.

And so America's awakening, when it came, was all the more painful and disorienting. "All that is solid melts into air," wrote Karl Marx during the turbulence of nineteenth-century industrialization. Many Americans felt the same after the attacks of September 11. One minute, we were enjoying the most privileged way of life in history. The next, terrorists had destroyed totemic symbols of our civilization and inflicted more deaths than the United States had suffered in a single day of combat since the Civil War. Suddenly Americans had learned the hard way: what foreigners think does matter.

THE DIFFERENCE BETWEEN AMERICA AND AMERICANS

What the United States does with this lesson is among the most important questions of our time, for Americans and foreigners alike. The initial response was, perhaps inevitably, military. After all, our country had been attacked in a vivid and horrifying way by sworn enemies whose spectacular assault left approximately three thousand civilians dead and caused countless billions of dollars' worth of economic losses. Any country so attacked would have the right to respond, and the Bush administration left little doubt that it planned to strike back hard. In the words of the Hollywood cowboy adage, "Shoot first, ask questions later." And the shooting went unexpectedly well in Afghanistan (if one leaves aside, as the United States government and media largely did, the deaths of Afghan civilians). The reaction in Europe was less enthusiastic, and the Arab world was downright dismayed; governments, but especially citizens, were distressed by the high civilian casualty figures and the prospect of future U.S. attacks against Iraq. But the fact remained that Afghanistan was liberated, the Taliban were routed, and bin Laden, as Bush boasted in December of 2001, "went from controlling a

country three months ago to now maybe controlling a cave."
But what about the "ask questions later" part of the cowboy adage? In the immediate aftermath of September 11, many average Americans recognized their ignorance of the outside world and moved to address it, emptying libraries and bookstores of volumes on Islam, the Middle East, and international affairs. The news media, after years of pandering to a lowest-common-denominator audience with stories about sex and celebrities, remembered that news was supposed to be *about* something and began to cover the outside world again. By the turn of the new year, however, as the war against terrorism seemed to be won and domestic scares over anthrax and airports had faded, old habits began to reassert themselves. In one sense a return to normalcy was welcome, but it raised the question of whether the newly inquiring mood after September 11 was a mere blip. Would America aim to understand the frightening new world of the twenty-first century, or be content merely to subdue it?

This question begs a distinction that will recur throughout this book. "I contain multitudes," wrote Walt Whitman, America's great poet, and it's true. There is no one American reality, and not merely because of the individualism that is our cardinal national trait; there is also the difference between Americans and America—that is, between the nation's 285 million citizens and the political, military, economic, and media institutions whose policies make up the nation's official posture in the world. While America and Americans can sometimes amount to the same thing, it is a mistake to automatically equate the two. As in most countries, the dominant institutions in the United States are run by elites whose views do not necessarily coincide with those of the general public. In fact, the gap between America's elites and its masses has been growing over the last quarter century as economic inequality intensifies, the wealthy and well-connected increasingly control the political process, and once proud news organizations are gobbled up by giant corporations whose only allegiance is to profits. At the same time, there are many values that most Americans share—President Bush enjoyed a 75 percent approval rating six months after September 11—and national unity is reinforced by the elites' control over the media that provide citizens with much of their information about the world. To oversimplify, the media *reflect* elite opinion but *shape* mass opinion.

Foreigners are often baffled that Americans, who are so adept at selling their products overseas, can simultaneously know so little about how they are perceived by others. But then few foreigners appreciate how poorly served Americans are by our media and educational systems—how narrow the range of information and debate is in the land of the free, another theme elaborated later in this book. For now, let a brief comparison of American and European media coverage after September 11 illustrate the point.

I was traveling in Europe in the weeks after the attacks. In the leading newspapers in Britain, Germany, France, Italy, and Spain I found plenty of news coverage that both sympathized with the horror inflicted upon my homeland and endorsed the right of the United States to retaliate militarily. But I also found lots of coverage that cautioned against a military response, drew a connection between the attacks and America's foreign policy, especially its perceived favoritism toward Israel, and urged attention to the root causes of terrorism, not just to sensational symbols like Osama bin Laden. "Bring the murderers to justice, but tackle the causes of these outrages," the September 14 *London Independent* opined in one typical commentary that urged reconsideration of U.S.-led sanctions against Iraq and America's reflexive support for Israel. In Germany, even the conservative tabloid *Bild* gave space to pacific as well as belligerent viewpoints; one article quoted a German businessman's letter to President Bush urging him to "punish the guilty, not the innocent . . . women and children of Afghanistan."

In the United States, by contrast, the news media's pronouncements were indistinguishable from the government's, and neither showed tolerance for anything less than full-throated outrage. At the Fox television network, correspondents wore American flag pins and anchor Brit Hume dismissed civilian deaths in Afghanistan as unworthy of news coverage. CNN chairman Walter Isaacson directed his U.S. staff not to mention civilian casualties in Afghanistan without at the same time recalling the Americans who died on September 11. (Tellingly, CNN did not impose such restrictions on its overseas broadcasts.) When the American media finally examined the question of how the United States appeared to the rest of the world, that richly complex subject was reduced to simplistic melodrama. The journalistic climate was such that anyone voicing the opinions expressed by the *London Independent* or *Bild* was accused of treasonous nonsense, as writer Susan Sontag discovered when she published an article in *The New Yorker* pointing out that American foreign policy had wreaked terrible damage on other countries in the past, so why all the surprise at being targeted itself now?

The American reaction was bound to be less measured than Europe's, of course; it was we who had been attacked, we who had suffered such grievous losses. But if Americans want to prevent further attacks in the future, we must realize that neither unleashing our fearsome military nor tightening domestic security will alone suffice, and that limiting discussion on supposedly patriotic grounds is positively unhelpful. We need at all costs to understand *why* this happened. Toward that end, we need to consider even those explanations that may not flatter us. We need to recognize, for example, that there is a crucial difference between explaining a given action and excusing that action. One can logically argue, as I would, that the United States in no way deserved the September 11 attacks (there is never any excuse for terrorism, period) and the perpetrators absolutely should be brought to justice, while adding that the attacks cannot be understood outside the context of American foreign policy and the resentment it has engendered.

There are numerous global hot spots where United States policies are controversial enough to feed the kind of rage that found murderous expression on September 11. Would bin Laden have launched his attack if the United States were not financing Israel's occupation of the Palestinian territories and stationing troops in Saudi Arabia? Quite possibly not, though I don't mean to suggest that Washington should grant terrorists veto power over its foreign policy. The point is, Americans need to have an honest discussion about our conduct overseas: Where is it wise? Where is it not? How often does it correspond to the values of democracy and freedom that we regularly invoke, and how important is it whether we practice what we preach?

AMERICA IS THE FUTURE

If Americans want a healthy relationship with the six billion people we share the planet with, we need to understand who those people are, how they live, what they think and why. This is not charity, it is self-interest. America may be protected by two oceans and the mightiest military in history, but we now know we are not untouchable. The United States sits atop an increasingly unequal world; 45 percent of humanity lives on less than two dollars a day. Peace and prosperity are unlikely under such conditions, as the CIA itself has warned. "Groups feeling left behind [by widening inequality] . . . will foster political, ethnic, ideological, and religious extremism, along with the violence that often accompanies it," an agency report forecast in 2000—as good a prediction of September 11 as one could want.

Foreigners have no less a stake in better understanding the United States. Thomas Jefferson wrote over two hundred years ago that "every man has two nations: his own, and France." Today, the second nation of every person on earth is the United States. The world is being made more American by the day, an obvious point to anyone who travels much. What the news media call globalization is in fact largely Americanization, and September 11 has not diminished the trend. But proximity does not equal understanding. At a time when they are increasingly intertwined through economics and technology, the United States and the rest of the world often gaze at each other in mutual incomprehension.

How, foreigners ask, can America be so powerful yet so naïve? So ignorant of foreign nations, peoples, and languages yet so certain it knows what's best for everyone? How can its citizens be so open and generous but its foreign policy so domineering? And why is it shocked when the objects of its policies grumble or even strike back?

What accounts for America's extraordinary optimism, its dynamic "can-do" spirit, its ceaseless pursuit of the "green light" F. Scott Fitzgerald invoked in *The Great Gatsby*? How can it put men on the moon and libraries onto computer chips but still debate the teaching of evolution in public schools and nearly impeach a president over an extramarital affair? How can Americans be so rich in material possessions but so lacking in family and community ties? So inundated with timesaving appliances yet perpetually stressed and hurried? How can the United States have given birth to uplifting cultural glories like jazz and rock and roll and socially resonant ethics like environmentalism yet be a cheerleader for vacuous celebrity, gratuitous violence, and ubiquitous luxury?

How can a nation famous as the land of opportunity be spawning a growing underclass for whom the American Dream has become a cruel myth? How could the world's proudest democracy descend to the chaos and corruption that stained the 2000 presidential contest? Was that shameful episode a harbinger of American decline, one now reinforced by the unspeakable tragedy of September 11? Or will the United States become once again the "shining city on a hill" that Ronald Reagan used to so proudly invoke?

These are difficult questions, and some Americans have no intention of facing them. The country is at war, in their view, and anyone who doesn't line up behind the commander-in-chief with his mouth shut should be put on the next plane to Baghdad. At times, the understandable surge of patriotism that followed September 11 has evolved into an unseemly superiority complex: a conviction that Americans are inherently more brave, caring, and generous than anyone else. It is "because we are Americans," as one book's title put it, that New York City firemen charged into the burning chaos of the World Trade Center to pull victims to safety—as if rescue workers in other countries were incapable of similar acts of courage and dedication.

Personally, I believe our country is strong enough to profit from a searching consideration of both its virtues and its vices. To any who nevertheless insist on accusing me of America-bashing, let me reply clearly, if only to disarm a slander that might otherwise be employed to dismiss this book: I do not hate America. I love America. As a journalist and writer, I feel blessed to live in the land of the First Amendment. I remain awed by the founding ideals of the United States; 225 years later, they survive as an inspiring prescription for, in Jefferson's majestic phrase, life, liberty, and the pursuit of happiness.

But America, I fear, has strayed from its founding ideals. September 11 left our people in a frightened, rally-round-the-flag mood. When we are ready to face facts again, we may see that our country was in crisis well before bin Laden's bombers set off on their mission of hate. Politically, we live in a democracy that barely deserves the name. Our government lectures others on how to run elections, yet most of our own citizens don't vote. Abdication of this basic civic responsibility may be rooted partly in the complacency that affluence can breed, but surely another cause is the alienation many Americans feel from a political system they correctly perceive as captive to the rich and powerful. Nor does our economy much resemble our democratic aspirations. In his 1831 classic, *Democracy in America,* Alexis de Tocqueville celebrated us as a nation where "great revolutions will become more rare" because our equality, he believed, was an ingrained tendency. Today, America is more and more divided between an elite that lives in cloistered luxury and a poor and middle class doomed to work hard but not get ahead. Meanwhile, in our foreign policy we say we stand for freedom and often we do, but we can be shamelessly hypocritical, siding with treacherous dictatorships that serve our perceived interests and overthrowing real democracies that do not.

The United States has much to be proud of, but it also has things to be sorry for. Why should Americans find this hard to admit? We will get along better with our neighbors, and vice versa, if we face up to this unsurprising but powerful fact. To insist that we ignore our faults—and label as a traitor anyone who refuses to be silent—is folly. Uncomfortable truths don't go away just because powerful voices want them shouted down. Nor is dissent un-American; quite the opposite. If one lesson of September 11 is that no nation is invulnerable in today's world, surely another is that America can no longer afford to ignore what the rest of the world thinks, even when—perhaps especially when—it is not laudatory.

Which brings me to the narrative map of this book. Each of its ten chapters offers a sort of dialogue between how foreigners and Americans perceive the United States. I organize the dialogue around a list of ten things that foreigners think about America that Americans usually don't talk about, as follows:

1. America is parochial and self-centered.
2. America is rich and exciting.
3. America is the land of freedom.
4. America is an empire, hypocritical and domineering.
5. Americans are naïve about the world.
6. Americans are philistines.
7. America is the land of opportunity.
8. America is self-righteous about its democracy.
9. America is the future.
10. America is out for itself.

I don't pretend to have all the answers about America. My homeland is too vast, too multifaceted, too full of surprises to

be easily summarized. The United States, wrote John Steinbeck, is "complicated, paradoxical, bullheaded, shy, cruel,
boisterous, unspeakably dear, and very beautiful." Still a
young nation, it remains (one of its greatest strengths) a work
in progress.

In a book as short as this, it is impossible to explore America in much detail. My purpose, rather, is to raise questions,
sometimes awkward ones, about America's behavior and beliefs at the dawn of the twenty-first century. Although this
book is based on extensive travel, reporting, and research, it is
more an opening argument than a definitive proof. I hope to
provoke thought and debate, and if readers don't disagree
with at least some of what I write, I probably haven't done my
job.

I know that parts of this book will be difficult for some
Americans to hear. As Tocqueville noted, we tend to "live in a
state of perpetual self-adoration. . . . Only strangers or experience may be able to bring certain truths to the Americans' attention." But as the global outpouring of sympathy following
September 11 illustrated, the rest of the world harbors great
affection for Americans along with other less enthusiastic feelings. And the majority of foreigners differentiate between
Americans as people—whom they generally like—and American power and foreign policy, which are far less admired.

Meanwhile, most foreigners recognize that it is in their
own interest to understand America as clearly as possible; after all, they all live in the Eagle's shadow. "I have wanted to
write an opinion article for the *New York Times* urging that
American elections be opened to foreigners, because what the
American government decides about economic policy, military action, and cultural mores affects me and all other people
around the world," Abdel Monem Said Aly, a journalist who

directs the Al-Ahram Center for Political and Strategic Studies in Cairo, told me. "When U.S. economic growth slows, we see the price of oil fall. When the U.S. stock market declines, the grants from the Ford Foundation to my center in Cairo decline."

Whatever the realm—economic, military, political, scientific, or cultural—the United States is the world's dominant nation. Its power is by no means absolute, but it is the decisive actor whose behavior, for better or worse, will shape the world that people everywhere will live in during the twenty-first century. Beldrich Moldan, a former environment minister of the Czech Republic, put it best. "As a European," he told me in Prague, "you may like the United States or not like the United States, but you know it's the future."

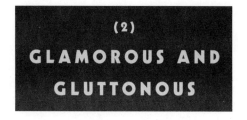

(2)

GLAMOROUS AND GLUTTONOUS

Mr. Ma spent the first ten years of his working life deep beneath the earth of northern China mining coal. Then, one day, he watched a runaway coal cart jump its tracks and mash a comrade's head as flat as a shovel. It was by no means the first grisly death Ma had witnessed underground, and he decided he'd had enough. As soon as he got back to the surface, he quit, vowing never to mine coal again.

Twelve years later, when I met him in December 1996, he still lived in his home village in Shanxi province, in the heart of China's vast coalfields, but now he was a budding capitalist. He ran a hole-in-the-wall restaurant with his wife and co-owned a blue van that he and a partner deployed as a taxi. The restaurant fronted on the road to Datong, an ugly, parched city ten miles away whose skyline was punctuated with dozens of smokestacks emitting endless plumes of thick black smoke. The public bus from Datong stopped just yards from the restaurant; outside, two donkeys were hitched to wagons filled with massive chunks of shiny black coal. Zhenbing, my interpreter, and I decided to stop in for lunch before touring the surrounding countryside.

White faces were rare enough in this area, but when Ma learned that I came from the United States, he called his wife out of the kitchen to come see. "This is what an American looks like," he enthused with a gleaming smile, looking me up and down as if I were a horse at auction. He sat down at my table and said, "I have many questions for you. We have the market economy in China now, but America has had the market economy a long time. You must tell me its secrets." Eyes twinkling, he concluded, "I want to be rich like you."

Ma was already a canny negotiator; when he learned that I wanted to visit nearby coal mines as part of my environmental research, he offered to serve as my tour guide and to include lunch in his fee. Before we headed out, I asked if there was a toilet I could use. With a proud smile, Ma beckoned me behind the restaurant to an outdoor row of low concrete stalls. None had doors, ceilings, or anything else but a hole in the center of the floor. Nor, as was common in rural China, was there water or soap for afterward.

I spent the rest of the afternoon with Mr. Ma, and he was amusing company, whether joking about reading between the lines of China's state-run media to guess whether supreme leader Deng Xiaoping was dead yet, or explaining how big a bribe he had to pay to get official permission to have a third child. I was surprised when, unprompted, he said he considered himself a lucky man. After all, he explained, he had escaped working in the mines, which most of his neighbors had not. Nor was he out scavenging coal along the roadside like countless others I had seen, scooping fallen fragments into baskets they balanced across weary shoulders for the walk home. At thirty-nine, Ma was also old enough to recall living through perhaps the largest act of mass murder in the twentieth century, the famine engineered by Mao Zedong from 1959 to 1962 that killed an estimated thirty million people and brought cannibalism and misery to much of rural China. "I remember that my father's sister brought us food she had hidden," he said quietly.

Ma answered every question I posed about China, and he asked plenty of his own about America. Most concerned material possessions: Did everyone there own a car? How many people lived in each house? How much land did they own? My replies triggered murmurs of wonder and unguarded admiration; clearly, Ma said, China had much to learn from the United States.

Finally, driving back to Datong as night was falling, Ma dared to broach the subject that apparently intrigued him most of all: sex. Is it true, he asked, that in America women sleep with men before marriage?

The news that, yes, this did sometimes happen unleashed a wail of envy. Ma seemed at once irritated and overjoyed; his wife, he implied, was the only sexual partner he had ever had. His questions came more quickly now: Did everyone in America do this? Had I done it? How many women could a man sleep with before marriage? Could a married man such as himself also sleep with other women? As my answers gradually made clear the yawning gap between America's relative sexual freedom and China's prudish restraint, Ma grew agitated. "This is what I thought," he exulted, banging his fist against the steering wheel. "America is the most rich, *and* it has the most fun." When at last he dropped Zhenbing and me at the hotel, he insisted I give him my business card. "Someday when I am rich," he said, "I will visit you in America. Without my wife."

"FUN, FUN, FUN"

We Americans have no idea how rich we are, but everyone else certainly does; it's often the first thing foreigners mention about the United States. There is, of course, also extensive poverty within the United States, especially among children, a condition I'll detail later in this book. But most of us take for granted modern bathrooms, hot showers, and unlimited water for cooking at the turn of a faucet; no walking to and from an unclean creek with buckets and building a fire first, as countless women in Africa, Asia, and South America still do every day. Nor do we think twice about jumping in one of our family's two or three cars and zipping off whenever we want, wherever we want; we disdain the buses, trains, and other forms of mass transit widely used even in affluent Japan and western Europe as too slow and inconvenient, and the walking that hundreds of millions of the world's poor rely upon is inconceivable to us; many of us will drive the two blocks to the corner store to pick up bread and milk. And that bread and milk, which are always fresh, only hint at the mind-boggling variety and volume of food and drink we have to choose from, whether in mammoth supermarkets whose shelves bulge with virtually every food imaginable no matter what time of year or where we live—strawberries in February, sea crabs in Denver—or in the restaurants that now receive 46 percent of all the money Americans spend on food per year.

Put another way, Americans don't realize how poor most other people in the world are. For most people on the planet, shopping is an exercise in penny-pinching prudence, not the compulsive hobby it has become for many Americans. Approximately one in every five human beings subsists on one dollar a day, a level of poverty which makes hunger and illness their frequent companions. According to the United Nations Food and Agriculture Organization, some 35,600 children die every day from "conditions of starvation"—that is, from the many illnesses that prey upon tiny bodies that go hungry day after day.

Americans are not unaware of world poverty—we're proud of sending food aid overseas—but we have little grasp of how beyond the human norm our own level of consumption is. It doesn't help that our news media have almost no interest in the outside world in general and the plight of the poor in particular; but neither do we get out and see for ourselves. The relatively few Americans who travel overseas generally confine themselves to zones of English-speaking comfort. Thus we remain oblivious to our extraordinary privilege.

At the same time, however, America's mystique in the eyes of the world is based on more than mere wealth. Mr. Ma is hardly the only foreigner who also associates the United States with excitement, adventure, and sheer pleasure.

When I had a minor fender bender amid the mad traffic of Palermo, the two young guys whose car I dented couldn't have been nicer. Waving off my fervent apologies, they asked where I was from, then replied in unison, "It's more beautiful than here, isn't it?" America is beautiful, I agreed, but I added that I had found Palermo's Monreale perhaps the most beautiful cathedral in all Europe. "America is also very big, no?" they continued, eyes bright with anticipation. Yes, I replied. "And there are many tall buildings and fancy restaurants and good dance clubs? Lots of fun things to do, right?" All true, I said. And so it went for another ten minutes, each of my answers leading them to nod and smile at one another and seek more details about a place they clearly imagined as the hippest scene ever.

It's too simple to think foreigners admire or envy America

just because it is rich. Plenty of other countries—in Europe, Asia, the Middle East—are also rich. The difference is that America is also glamorous, cool, and exciting. Its high-throttle energy, joined with its unabashed ambition, creates a dynamo of ceaseless forward motion, as anyone who knows New York City can well attest. Its awesome scale and beauty, especially in the West—the Grand Canyon, Yosemite, the wild reaches of Alaska—are at once exhilarating and humbling. Sometimes dangerous, always confident, never predictable, America is a fast, wide-open place where money is the scorecard and the sky is no limit. Even as worldly an observer as the French writer Simone de Beauvoir was smitten. In America, she wrote during a visit in 1947, "one has the inspired feeling that anything is possible."

That optimism was present from the nation's beginning, and it helps explain how the United States grew rich in the first place. Americans were an adventurous people, the philosopher George Santayana explained, because "the discovery of the new world exercised a sort of selection among the inhabitants of Europe. . . . The fortunate, the deeply rooted, and the lazy remained at home; the wilder instincts or dissatisfaction of others tempted them beyond the horizon." In his *Letters from an American Farmer*, published in 1782, French immigrant J. Hector St. John de Crèvecoeur noted, "A European, when he first arrives, seems limited in his intentions, as well as in his views; but he very suddenly alters his scale; two hundred miles formerly appeared a very great distance, it is not but a trifle; he no sooner breathes our air than he forms schemes, and embarks on designs he never would have thought of in his own country."

The new nation's dynamism was rooted in both physical and philosophical traits, including a sometimes ruthless disregard for its religious ideals. "America is the only great nation of modern times whose history is also the history of the three shaping forces of the modern Western world—*industrialism* as a technology, *capitalism* as a way of organizing it, and *democracy* as a way of running both," the late historian Max Lerner pointed out. "The American tradition, woven from these elements, took on their dynamism." America was also exceedingly well endowed with natural resources, which white settlers promptly seized from native inhabitants. As early as 1827, a visiting Scotsman, Captain Thomas Hamilton, could see the great fortunes that lay ahead: "No man can contemplate the vast internal resources of the United States—the varied productions of their soil, the unparalleled extent of river communication, the inexhaustible stores of coal and iron which are spread even on the surface—and doubt that the Americans are destined to become a great manufacturing nation." Agriculture blossomed first, however. Cotton picked by black slaves was the nation's leading export until the Civil War ended slavery in 1865.

"America is possessed of a great store of energy, and therefore everything in it, the good and the bad, develops with greater rapidity than anywhere else," Maxim Gorky, the Russian writer, argued in 1906. Indeed, it took the United States just a century and a quarter after its founding in 1776 to become the largest economy in the world. By the end of World War I, in 1918, the American economy was larger than those of Britain, France, Germany, and Russia combined. World War II greatly extended its lead; the United States was the only economy that came out of the war healthier rather than destroyed, setting the stage for its explosion into a prosperity unprecedented in human history.

America's golden era lasted from the end of the war in 1945 until the OPEC oil embargo of 1973. The embargo's role in closing the era was no coincidence, for cheap oil, and the love affair with the automobile it encouraged, were crucial to the era's hypergrowth. After World War II, the car consolidated its hold on the national transportation system, thanks to a combination of corporate villainy (a consortium including General Motors, Standard Oil, and Firestone Tire and Rubber secretly bought up bus and trolley systems around the country, then shut them down to destroy the car's competition), government subsidy (Washington in 1956 launched what President Dwight Eisenhower called "the largest public works program in history" to crisscross the nation with superhighways), and the car's own appeal as a convenient, exciting form of mobility. More cars in turn made possible the era's greatest engine of economic growth—the creation of suburbs, a development with huge social, environmental, and cultural implications as well. All the new roads, houses, schools, and other supporting infrastructure built to shift tens of millions of Americans from cities to suburbs gave the economy an enormous and continuing stimulus, boosting profits and wages alike for decades.

The high-consumption lifestyle Americans now take for granted took hold during this golden era (though its origins reach back to the rise of consumer goods production and advertising in the early 1900s). Two-car families became the norm: one car for dad's job, another for mom's errands. Labor-saving appliances were suddenly everywhere: dishwashers, vacuum cleaners, electric can openers, clothes washer-and-dryers. Radio was eclipsed virtually overnight as the nation fell in love with television, whose commercials only whetted people's appetites for more consumer goods. Creature comforts proliferated, as did marketing surveys; Americans came to be identified as consumers more than as citizens.

No place epitomized the era's attractions more than the Golden State itself, California. Talk about paradise! As Hollywood portrayed it, California was an endless summer of romance and self-indulgence, a magical place where living was easy and all dreams came true. The sun, the beach, the bodies, the cars to bring them all together (convertibles, of course)—what more could you ask? It was "Fun, Fun, Fun," as the Beach Boys song put it, and it drew young people in particular from across the nation. Indeed, California's appeal then was like America's appeal today—the appeal of a movie star: charismatic, extravagant, spoiled, unforgettable.

SHARING ENVIRONMENTAL SPACE

In a world of extreme and growing inequality, America stands as the ultimate symbol of wealth and ease. "The richest fifth of the world's people consume 86 percent of all goods and services, while the poorest fifth are left with just over one percent," according to the United Nations Human Development Report of 1999. Humanity has been divided into rich and poor for thousands of years, but a crucial part of the dynamic has changed: television makes today's poor much more aware of just how poor they are, and of how much luxury they are missing. Their varied responses to this awareness, and by extension to America, illuminate what may well be the greatest challenge of the new millennium: to combat the poverty that afflicts the majority of the human family (and provides such a fertile breeding ground for terrorism, disease, and other threats to rich and poor alike) while at the same time preserving the natural ecosystems that make life possible in the first place.

"If you walked down the street here and asked people what their immediate impression of America is," a young engineer named Hany told me over lunch in Cairo in June 2001, "most of them would say, 'That's the easy life I want.'" This perspective is shared by countless other poor people around the world. Relatively few of those I have met seem to resent America's wealth. Rather, as Mr. Ma of China said, they want to know its secrets and are ready to work for its rewards.

Some foreigners do take a harsher view, condemning the United States (and other members of the world's comfortable class) for indifference to their suffering. "Sometimes we think outsiders come here to laugh at us," Jok, a local relief official, told me in 1992 in southern Sudan amid the starvation and misery of a decades-long civil war. "They take pictures, ask questions, make notes. Then they go back to their comfortable lives and nothing changes. . . . But we are still here." Once, in St. Petersburg, I gently chastised a Russian friend for smoking so many cigarettes; didn't he care about his health? He gave me a long, scornful look, took another drag of his cigarette, and said, "I make deal with you, Mark. You give me your American passport, you live here and I live there for six months. Then we see who is smoking the most cigarettes."

There is a minority in many countries that not only admire America's way of life but are copying it outright. Sport utility vehicles, the gas-guzzling behemoths that account for half of all new car sales in the United States, are now sighted on the streets of European and Asian capitals as well. To many foreigners, however, America's consumption patterns look excessive, even silly. "In the big shopping malls in the United States, you find hundreds of brands and sizes of pasta, soap, chewing gum, whatever," the Egyptian engineer told me.

"I have to laugh. Surely five or six kinds of toothpaste are enough."

But the global effect of American consumerism is no joke. With 5 percent of the earth's population, the United States is responsible for approximately 25 percent of humanity's environmental footprint—that is, its consumption of timber, minerals, and other resources; its destruction of rain forests, wetlands, and endangered species; and its production of such pollutants as the dioxins that poison water supplies and the carbon dioxide that drives global climate change. This 5 to 25 percent discrepancy exists because Americans consume so much more per capita than foreigners do. Thus when the United States refuses to limit its huge appetites—for example, when the Bush administration unilaterally rejects the Kyoto protocol on global warming on the (specious) grounds that reducing greenhouse gas emissions would harm the American economy, and when Congress votes down an increase in automobile fuel efficiency that would lower U.S. emissions more than Kyoto would—it looks like the selfishness of a glutton. "Americans are individualists, and you consume the same way," said the Egyptian engineer. "You do what is good for you and you don't care about anyone else."

It's ironic that the United States is now viewed as an environmental renegade, for it is we who gave birth to the modern environmental ethic. In 1872, America invented the national park—later hailed by James Bryce, British ambassador to the United States, as the best idea America ever had—when President Ulysses S. Grant signed a bill designating over two million acres of Wyoming as Yellowstone National Park. America also pioneered the concept of wilderness areas, where any human activity that might compromise utter wildness was banned. In 1962, publication of Rachel Carson's *Silent Spring* initiated a new phase of the environmental movement, focused on protection against industrial pollution. An activated citizenry soon forced Washington to pass clean air and water laws that have become models for countries throughout the world. How unfortunate that over the past twenty years the United States has compromised this legacy through unbridled consumerism and backsliding.

The American style of life is attractive, but if all six billion people on earth shared it, it would take three more planets to provide all the raw materials required and absorb all the pollution produced. Since this earth is the only one we have, humanity must somehow share the existing environmental space. Better technology—improved energy efficiency, a rapid shift to solar and other non-fossil fuels, and similar transformations in agriculture, transportation, construction, and other sectors—can tremendously reduce humanity's environmental footprint. But technology can do only so much. As billions of poor people strive to improve their lot in the years ahead, our collective environmental footprint will inevitably increase—unless there is a corresponding reduction in consumption by the wealthy, who are now occupying much more than their fair share of environmental space.

Where this dynamic plays out most dramatically is in America's relationship with China. On a per capita basis, China consumes 10 percent as much energy as the United States. Yet even under the supposedly environmental presidency of Bill Clinton, the United States refused to accept mandatory greenhouse gas reductions unless China and other large poor countries did the same. But it is the rich nations whose earlier industrialization is most responsible for climate change, the Chinese point out, so why hold poor nations equally responsible?

"The Americans say China is the straw that breaks the camel's back on greenhouse gas emissions," Zhou Dadi, deputy director general of the State Planning Commission's Energy Research Institute, told me in Beijing. "But we say, 'Why don't you take some of your heavy load off the camel first?' If the camel belongs to America, fine, we'll walk. But the camel does not belong to America. . . . China will insist on the per capita principle. What else are we supposed to do? Go back to no heat in winter? Impossible."

This was no rhetorical flourish. Zhenbing, my interpreter in China, grew up very poor in a small village about 120 miles northwest of Beijing. In a climate as cold as Boston's or Berlin's, his family could burn only dried leaves or straw to warm their mud hut. "Often the straw was not enough," Zhenbing recalled, "so the inside wall of the hut became white with icy waterdrops, like frozen snow." Only after China initiated economic reforms in 1980 did families like Zhenbing's begin to acquire enough money to buy coal.

Multiply Zhenbing's story by the nearly one and a half billion people who live in China and you see why China has become an environmental superpower second only to the United States. The extra coal that Chinese people burned over the past two decades to prevent white walls in winter has had horrific environmental consequences. Nine of the ten most air-polluted cities in the world are in China. Nearly one in every three deaths there is linked to air and water pollution. Nor is the outside world immune. China's modernization leaves it poised to overtake the United States as the world's leading emitter of greenhouse gases by approximately 2020.

As environmental superpowers, China and the United States each exercise what amounts to veto power over the world's progress toward a sustainable future. Each nation accounts for such a large share of global consumption that international attempts to reverse greenhouse gas emissions or other harmful trends simply can't succeed without their cooperation. China's environmental heft derives mainly from its gargantuan population; one in every four humans is Chinese. The United States casts its long environmental shadow mainly because of its lavish consumption patterns (while also having the world's fourth-largest population). Chinese outnumber Americans more than five to one, but the average American consumes fifty-three times more goods and services. In China, there is one car per every five hundred people; in the United States, one car per every two.

ADDICTED TO SHOPPING

The car is only the most obvious symbol of America's tendency to consume as if there were no tomorrow. In summer we crank the air-conditioning to the max, chilling our homes, stores, and movie theaters to temperatures that would make us shiver and complain in winter. Children and grown-ups alike love their toys and can't wait to buy more—cameras and then video cameras, televisions and then DVDs, skis and then snowboards—all of which get discarded for newer models. We spent $535 billion on entertainment in 1999, more than the combined GNPs of the world's forty-five poorest nations. Our restaurants serve portions far larger than any one person can eat. The soft drinks sold by convenience stores are as ludicrously oversized as their Extreme Gulp and Super-Jumbo names imply, and their containers soon join the flood of garbage that pours into landfills every day in a nation where virtually everything is overwrapped and thrown away after a single use. The vast majority of Americans say they care a lot about the environment, and many prove their virtue by recycling bottles, cans, and newspaper. But recycling is a losing battle unless underlying patterns change. America recycled three times as much paper in 1999 as in 1975, but soaring consumption rates meant that the total volume of wastepaper still increased.

Individual Americans bear some responsibility for this orgy of consumption, but it's not our fault we live in an advertising-saturated culture that is forever seducing, cajoling, even outright demanding that we do our patriotic part and buy that new home entertainment system. Americans are bombarded by advertisements from the time we wake up to the time we go to sleep (and no doubt enterprising advertising executives will eventually figure out how to invade our slumbering hours as well). Approximately one in every three minutes of American television is advertising. Children are especially targeted; establish brand loyalty early and you gain a customer for life. And there is no such thing as too young; in 1998 marketers started targeting one-year-olds. An executive for the media giant Time Warner conceded that this was "vaguely evil," but business is business. By age seven, an average American child watches twenty-seven hours of television a week—nearly four hours a day—and sees an incredible twenty thousand commercials a year.

And consuming is made easy by the American economy's growing reliance on debt. Banks offer consumers a staggering four billion credit cards per year, an average of fifteen cards for every man, woman, and child in the United States. "Charge it" is becoming our national motto. But the bills eventually come due; personal bankruptcies increased 70 percent between 1995 and 1999.

No wonder the shopping mall has replaced the church and town square as the center of our social life. When the American writer Bill Bryson returned to the United States in 1996 after living in England for twenty years, he was awed by the friendliness and generosity of his fellow Americans—the week his family moved in, perfect strangers dropped off bottles of wine, home-cooked meals, even living room furniture—but he was dismayed by the culture's wanton consumerism. Trying to order a simple cup of coffee one morning before boarding an airplane, Bryson was bewildered by how long it took the line to move, until he got to the front and discovered that he, like his predecessors, had to choose among dozens of variations—mocha, cappuccino, decaf; skim, whole, or 2 percent milk—before being served; the clerk literally could not grasp that all he wanted was a black coffee. A trip to the mall revealed the same excess, now expanded to include scores of stores and all manner of unnecessary junk. Meanwhile, his fellow citizens seemed content to drift, as if sleepwalking, from one consumption opportunity to the next. "This abundance of choice . . . in a strange way actually breeds dissatisfaction," Bryson later wrote. "The more there is, the more people crave. . . . We appear to have created a society in which the principal pastime is grazing through retail establishments looking for things—textures, shapes, flavors—not before encountered."

Besides the millions of individuals who are addicted to shopping, the nation as a whole depends on shopping to keep the economy humming. Consumer spending accounts for two-thirds of domestic economy activity. If people stop or even slow their shopping, businesses falter, workers are laid off, recession looms. The danger was starkly illustrated when the September 11 terror attacks threatened to bring down not only the World Trade Center but the national economy as well. It was bad enough that September 11 left many Americans too frightened to fly, thus slashing revenues for airlines, hotels, and other travel-related industries. But the attacks also engendered a new seriousness among the American people, a turning away from self-indulgence and material things in favor of spiritual values and service to others. The consequent drop in consumer spending turned the economy's preexisting decline into an outright recession. Alarmed political leaders began telling the public that respect for the dead was all very well, but it was time to get out there and spend money. "America: Open for Business" trumpeted the red, white, and blue logos that were suddenly displayed on shop windows and billboards across the United States. As a national motto, it lacked the grandeur of Roosevelt's "We have nothing to fear but fear itself" or Kennedy's "Ask not what your country can do for you," but it did reflect the American faith that buying and selling are the path to happiness.

"I can't go over to Afghanistan. What I can do is make sure that we have the best Santa in town," said Linda Wardell, the assistant general manager of the Polaris shopping mall in Columbus, Ohio, a city known as a bellwether of Middle America. A massive cathedral to consumerism, the 1.5 million–square–foot mall opened its doors on October 25, just in time for the holiday rush. The Christmas season is the essential annual stimulus for American capitalism; the single biggest shopping day of the year comes, ironically, the day after the Thanksgiving holiday. But in recent years, complaints about the commercialization of Christmas—especially the increase in manipulative advertising pressuring consumers to buy, buy, buy or look like a Scrooge—have increased. A poll commissioned by the Center for a New American Dream, a public interest group that advocates responsible consumption, found that 62 percent of Americans resent the stress they feel toward Christmas shopping and 47 percent emerge from the holidays saddled with large debts; of those, one in five is still repaying the debt the following fall, when the cycle begins anew.

Is the souring of the Christmas holiday a sign that America has become too rich for its own good? In a country that has always worshiped wealth and its pursuit, merely to pose such a question is blasphemy, but the evidence is hard to ignore. Americans' very bodies are testaments to bloat and sloth. Dr. David Satcher, the surgeon general of the United States, warned in December 2001 that 60 percent of our adults are overweight or obese (a five-foot-six adult is overweight at 160 pounds, obese at 190). He blamed lifestyles empty of exercise but filled with junk food, and he calculated that 300,000 Americans a year die as a result—more than die from alcohol, drugs, firearms, and motor vehicles combined.

Likewise, our unbridled fondness for cars—the vehicle population of the United States grew six times as fast as the human population did between 1969 and 1995—is coming back to haunt us. Despite cleaner individual cars, the pollution of the overall auto fleet causes 30,000 deaths and 120,000 premature deaths every year, mainly among the very young and very old, whose lungs are most sensitive. Asthma now afflicts one of every fifteen Americans under age eighteen. When traffic restrictions were imposed during the 1996 Olympic Games in Atlanta, the decline in air pollution led to a 42 percent drop in hospitalizations for asthma. Traffic jams also cost $100 billion a year in lost productivity, not to mention the boredom and stress inflicted on the drivers involved. In Los Angeles, symbol of the California dream, "drivers now spend an average of seven working days a year sitting motionless in traffic," the *New York Times* has reported. And the problem is bound to get worse, if only because all American teenagers assume it their right to own a car. Yet even killer congestion may not convince Americans to drive less; after all, traffic jams are always *other* people's fault.

MORE FUN, LESS STUFF

It serves little purpose for Americans to feel guilty over how rich the United States is, but we are fools if we remain oblivious to how privileged we are. In a world that is overwhelmingly poor, we are incredibly, often wastefully, rich. America's wealth has enormous consequences, but we are barely aware of it, never mind discussing what to do about it. This is not smart. Neither is it compassionate. It even runs counter to our immediate self-interest in living healthier lives.

There is something ignoble about consuming so thoughtlessly when so many others have so little, and Americans should not be surprised when our behavior triggers the same feelings the wealthy have attracted throughout history: envy, admiration, even worship, but also jealousy, resentment, and the backlash they can trigger. At the very least, our apparent indifference to the plight of the poor kindles their determination to get as rich as we are, often by making the same mistakes. The American approach to consumption, which is decidedly *not* the same thing as our standard of living, is environmentally ruinous. Yet because our "shop till you drop" lifestyle looks like fun, others want to copy it. On a finite planet, this is a recipe for disaster. Yet how can we expect people in China—like Mr. Ma and Zhenbing—or anywhere else to restrain themselves when we balk at even the slightest cutbacks for ourselves?

Some Americans, especially from the corporate sector, complain that any talk of limits on consumption is dangerous drivel that will leave us shivering in the dark. Nonsense. It is our current consumption habits that are killing us through obesity and stress, not to mention distancing us from what is truly important in life. There is a big difference between comfort and excess; we could maintain a very comfortable standard of living while radically reforming the way we consume. We could begin by launching a Green Deal program, modeled on our race to the moon in the 1960s, that would enable us to kick our oil habit within ten years. By spending not more but more wisely, a government-led, market-driven Green Deal would shift federal subsidies away from oil and other environmental dead ends and bring solar power, hydrogen fuel cells, and mass transit on line while boosting jobs and profits alike.

And shouldn't Americans also think about consuming less in absolute terms? After all, when one is dining on steak and ice cream twice a day, slimming down is the wisdom of survival, not a diet of sacrifice. Nor need slimming down diminish the glamour traditionally associated with the United States, for surely our mystique is rooted in our spirit, not our credit cards. Long before twenty-four-hour shopping malls and fast-food franchises blighted our landscape and television turned many of us into couch potatoes, the United States was the home of Elvis Presley, Greenwich Village, Amelia Earhart, Delta blues, Ella Fitzgerald, San Francisco, Muhammad Ali, the Wild West, Mark Twain, the Grand Ole Opry, Babe Ruth, the Great Plains, Bob Dylan, the Cotton Club, and countless other people and places that inspired foreigners with yearning and made natives proud to be American. Money is nice in its place, but the magic of life derives from a deeper source, as September 11 led many Americans to remember. Weaning ourselves from excessive materialism won't be easy, but a motto emerging from the voluntary simplicity movement hints at the potential rewards: "More fun, less stuff."

TAKING FREEDOM
FOR GRANTED

Mohammed Ghaly is a cripple now. His job as a salesman used to take him all over Egypt, even to Libya, until one day a car swerving through Cairo's chaotic traffic jumped the curb and crushed his left leg. At age fifty-one, he now needs crutches to get around, and rarely leaves his neighborhood in the Islamic Quarter. He spends most days visiting with friends in the local tea shops, reading newspapers, playing backgammon, passing the time.

On the day he meets me, it is ferociously hot, nearly 105 degrees Fahrenheit. He sits on a rickety chair on the shady side of one of the many unpaved alleys near Al-Azhar, Cairo's oldest university and most famous mosque, where the day before I had seen hundreds gather in low, dark rooms to study the Koran, pray, and prostrate themselves before Allah. The alley echoes with shouts and murmurs from the bustling local bazaar. Long, flowing robes of crimson, gold, and turquoise hang from second-floor windows while an intoxicating mix of fragrances wafts from a corner shop where turmeric, dates, and other delicacies are piled in squat burlap sacks. A teenage boy strides purposefully through the crowd, carrying a tray with four glasses of tea, which he sets on a small table between Ghaly and me. It is June 2001.

As my interpreter starts to explain why I am here, Ghaly seems eager to show he knows some English. "Welcome to Cairo," he interjects with a smile. "I hope you enjoy the visit." I begin with my usual question: "What is the first thing that you think of when I say 'America'?" Ghaly waits for the translation and then, without hesitation, gives a short, forceful reply in his native tongue: "Democracy and freedom."

"Really?" I say, somewhat taken aback. "Most Egyptians say Israel."

Ghaly smiles. "That is because they don't like that America always stands on the side of Israel and against the Arabs and the Palestinians. And I agree on this point. The American government is good inside of America but not good outside." He takes a sip of tea. "But we know that some Americans also don't like what their government does [overseas], because America is a free country and people there have good minds and can think for themselves."

After the harsh condemnations of the United States I had heard earlier that morning from the three retired terrorists, I was surprised by Ghaly's remarks. In retrospect, I shouldn't have been. I've often heard similar praise of America over the years, especially in countries where freedom and democracy are distant dreams.

During six weeks in China in 1996–97, I interviewed Dai Qing, a prominent journalist who described how she had been jailed and kept under house arrest simply for writing articles that raised doubts about the infamous Three Gorges Dam project. Back in the United States, I questioned Wei Jinsheng, the courageous Democracy Wall dissident who had just been freed into exile after eighteen years behind bars, where he had endured the loss of all his teeth, subfreezing cells, and countless beatings because he had insisted on basic rights that Americans take for granted. Nowadays, Chinese have more freedom in the personal sphere—choosing jobs, mates, and where to live—but any who press for real democracy remain at risk. Although elections have been introduced at the village level, party bosses remain in control, employing strong-arm tactics to enable their looting of public revenues.

In Russia in 1995, former navy submarine commander Aleksandr Nikitin was jailed for publishing publicly available information about the navy's dumping of radioactive materials in the Baltic Sea. Nikitin finally won his freedom in 1999, and when I interviewed him he was quick to say that he had triumphed largely because he had international support unavailable to average Russians. Individual Russians feel "absolutely helpless" when menaced by the state security apparatus, the nation's human rights commissioner testified in 2002. That same year, journalist Grigory Pasko met a fate similar to Nikitin's, and for a similar "crime": four years in jail for revealing already public information.

Need I add that such injustices are not confined to (former) Communist countries? In Kenya, I spoke with activist Wangari Maathai about her ingenious Green Belt program—paying poor women to plant trees, thus fighting poverty, deforestation, and women's inequality all at once. Six weeks later, she and others marching in downtown Nairobi for free elections were beaten by goons reportedly dispatched by the dictatorial president, Daniel arap Moi. In Brazil, I was escorted to the secret creekside hideaway of landless peasants whose leaders were being arrested or shot for daring to squat on unused farmland. I could recount depressingly similar firsthand stories from Zimbabwe, Turkey, and Mexico, and anyone who wishes can find more of them via the literature or web sites of Amnesty International and other human rights groups. No wonder America looks like paradise to some foreigners.

For his part, Ghaly saw evidence of state repression every day in Cairo—not just in Egypt's media (all television and radio networks are state-run) and political systems (elections are barely a formality) but also in the regime's treatment of his friends and neighbors. After Ghaly and I had been talking for twenty minutes or so, a delivery truck approached from the right, sputtering the diesel fumes that make Cairo's air such a noxious soup of poisons. The alley was so narrow the truck had to inch forward to pass, a task the driver managed with, I thought, considerable skill. But one of Ghaly's associates burst into a deranged tirade, pounding on the truck's side before his friends dragged him off and gave the driver an apologetic wave onward. The same guy had shouted at me earlier when I declined his offer of a soda to go with my tea. Ghaly saw my puzzled face and explained, through my interpreter, "Do not think bad of Amir. His mind was ruined by prison. As a student, he got involved with a group demanding political reform. It was a religious group, not violent. He was sent to jail, no court. When he came out twenty years later, he was like this."

"I do not think this would happen in America," Ghaly continued. "There, if you want to say anything, you have the freedom to say it. You respect the views of others and they respect you. This is very important. America was the first country in the world to do this, I think."

WHAT'S SO PATRIOTIC ABOUT THE "USA PATRIOT ACT"?

After its wealth, America is most admired around the world for its freedoms. And with good reason: the establishment of the United States was a milestone of monumental importance in humanity's long, continuing journey from minority to majority rule. When George Washington, Benjamin Franklin, James Madison, Thomas Jefferson, and the other founders of the United States asserted in our Declaration of Independence that "all men are created equal" (and with typically American impudence claimed that this "truth" was "self-evident"), it marked a radical break from the past. In 1776, Europe was still ruled by kings, princes, and popes, and, except for a tiny oligarchy, the public enjoyed neither freedom from coercion nor much say in communal matters. The founders insisted that another, more inclusive future was possible, and Americans have spent the last 225 years reaping the benefits of their vision. The political, religious, and legal freedoms that are the birthright of every American are a rightful source of both national pride and foreign admiration.

But the reality of American freedom is more complex than some foreigners realize. Three months after I interviewed Ghaly, the United States was convulsed by the terror attacks of September 11, and suddenly the notion that Americans were free to say whatever they liked went out the window. Two newspaper columnists who dared to question why President Bush spent September 11 shuttling from one airfield to another instead of returning to Washington were fired overnight. When Jerry Falwell and Pat Robertson, two well-known leaders of the Christian right, agreed on television that the attacks had been punishment for America's supposed descent into homosexuality and godless decadence, the ensuing public uproar quickly led them to withdraw the remarks. Bill Maher, a television personality, also had to publicly apologize after commenting that, whatever else the terrorists were, they weren't cowards. Appearing before Congress in December, Attorney General John Ashcroft warned that any lawmaker who questioned his proposed restrictions on civil liberties was "only aid[ing] terrorists." Congressional Republicans likewise accused Senate Majority Leader Tom Daschle of giving "aid and comfort" to the enemy—the legal definition of treason—after he dared suggest that the nation needed to hear more about the Bush administration's desire to attack Iraq and oust dictator Saddam Hussein.

The climate of intimidation was such that the most radical assault mounted on the United States Constitution in decades became law with scarcely a peep of protest from either the political class or the general public. On October 25, 2001, President Bush signed into law the "USA PATRIOT Act," an Orwellian phrase if ever there was one. Among its many extraordinary provisions, the law canceled habeas corpus rights for noncitizens (which amounted to twenty million people in the United States); the attorney general was now authorized to detain indefinitely any noncitizen that he and he alone deemed a threat to the national security. It allowed government agents to search a citizen's house without notifying that citizen, and it expanded the government's ability to wiretap not only telephone but Internet communications, giving the government access to a person's e-mail and bank and credit card records. Federal agents could also seize public library records to check what people were reading. Separately, the Justice Department asserted the right to monitor conversations between criminal suspects and their lawyers. Other new laws gave the CIA the right to spy on Americans, authorized the attorney general on his sole discretion to designate domestic groups as terrorist organizations, and lowered the legal threshold for obtaining a search warrant from "probable cause" to "relevant to an ongoing criminal investigation." Meanwhile, the president declared by executive fiat that any noncitizen he considered a suspected terrorist could be tried by a military tribunal rather than by an ordinary court; the tribunal would operate in secret, could impose the death penalty, and would not be subject to judicial appeal.

The people's representatives in Congress passed the "USA PATRIOT Act" by overwhelming margins. The Senate approved it by a vote of 98 to 1; in the House, only 66 of the 435 members voted against it. As the lone Senate dissenter, Wisconsin Democrat Russell Feingold, explained, "It is crucial that civil liberties in this country be preserved. Otherwise I'm afraid terror will win this battle without firing a shot." In the House, Representative Dennis Kucinich, Democrat of Ohio, went further. The "USA PATRIOT Act" and other steps taken by the Bush administration, Kucinich argued in a speech in December, revoked half of the ten amendments in the Bill of Rights: the First Amendment right to freedom of speech and assembly; the Fourth Amendment prohibition against unreasonable search and seizure; the Fifth Amendment right to due process; the Sixth Amendment right to a prompt public trial; and the Eighth Amendment protection against cruel and unusual punishment.

There was virtually no discussion, much less criticism, of this extraordinary expansion of government secrecy and police power when it mattered most—before the bill was passed and signed into law. Ventilating the proposed measures and subjecting them to reasoned debate might have helped separate the wheat from the chaff, illuminating what sorts of changes would really improve intelligence gathering and security preparedness and how to do so without sacrificing essential freedoms. But there was no such debate. One prominent Washington journalist, who asked to remain nameless, told me after the fact that "there was no time [for news coverage]. They rushed [the bill] through before the press could focus on it." It is true the bill was introduced on September 19 and signed on October 25, which is lightning-fast by Washington standards. Nevertheless, journalists had five weeks to analyze the law and bring its provisions to public attention. For people who face deadlines every day, that was plenty of time.

And what a difference outspoken news coverage might have made! The exception proves the point: when journalists did finally wake up, they trained their fire on Bush's military tribunals, which conservative columnist William Safire lambasted as "kangaroo courts" that gave Bush "dictatorial power." Other critics pointed out that such courts would damage America's reputation overseas and thus sacrifice the moral high ground in the war on terrorism. Sustained media criticism led the administration to modify its proposal somewhat; the revised tribunals would not operate in total secrecy or prohibit all appeals.

The most worrisome aspect of all this was not the government's restrictions on freedom, as chilling as they were, but the public's apparent acceptance of those restrictions. Opinion polls suggested that more than 70 percent of Americans were willing to give up some freedoms during the war on terrorism (which, it was said, would last decades). Some worried that the government would excessively restrict average Americans' civil liberties, but tolerance for actions aimed at immigrants and minorities was high. A Gallup poll found that

82 percent of respondents supported increased government power to detain even legal immigrants; 49 percent favored identification cards for Arab-Americans. A Harris CNN/Time poll found that 31 percent of respondents thought that Arab-Americans should be detained in camps.

Thus did both the Bush administration and a sizable minority of the citizenry flirt with replaying one of the most shameful episodes in modern American history: the internment in camps of some 110,000 Japanese-Americans, as well as 11,000 German-Americans and 3,000 Italian-Americans, during World War II for no other reason than their ethnic backgrounds. To his credit, President Bush spoke out in the days immediately following September 11, urging Americans to show tolerance toward American Muslims. But meanwhile his administration was actively violating the rights of some twelve hundred noncitizens who were hauled into custody and detained without charges, just as the World War II internees had been. Not only did the Bush administration deny these detainees access to lawyers, it refused to identify them. An additional five thousand people within Arab-American or Muslim communities were singled out for police interrogation. "We're an open society," the president declared, "but we're at war."

AMERICANS DON'T KNOW
OUR OWN HISTORY

Why have Americans raised so little fuss about this assault on our liberties? Have we enjoyed so much freedom for so long that we have grown complacent about losing it? Panicked by the terror attacks, are we now willing to trade freedom for security? We have a history of accepting restrictions on our liberties during times of perceived threat; there was broad support for the Palmer Raids in the 1920s and McCarthyism in the 1950s. But how aware are we of the scale of the current crackdown? James Madison once observed that "a people who mean to be their own governors must arm themselves with the power which knowledge gives." Unfortunately, Americans get our knowledge about the government from news media that have largely failed to highlight the urgency of the threat. But we are also handicapped by a more deep-seated ignorance.

The sad fact is, we don't know our own history. The latest evidence came in May 2002, after some 23,000 students took a history exam that is periodically administered by the federal government. Among the multiple-choice questions that high school seniors had to answer, one asked if the "Harlem Renaissance" referred to urban renewal projects in the 1960s, African-American political gains during Reconstruction, a religious revival in the 1950s, or—the correct answer—African-American achievements in art, literature, and music in the 1920s. Only 10 percent of twelfth-graders—students who had reached or soon would reach voting age—scored well enough on the exam to be considered proficient, a performance that educator Diane Ravitch deplored as "truly abysmal." (A similar test in 1995 found that half of all twelfth-graders were unaware of the Cold War.)

Americans' ignorance of our history goes beyond mere facts and figures to include a deeper conceptual blindness: we fail to appreciate that the freedoms we enjoy today exist only because our ancestors struggled to bring them into being—by working to end slavery, to extend voting rights to nonwhite, nonpropertied, and female citizens, to resist McCarthyism and other expansions of police power, and so forth. Our history demonstrates that freedom is a work in progress, and that it is always provisional. It can be lost if not vigilantly defended.

Much of our ignorance stems from how we learn history in the United States. Rather than the full, tangled truth about our past, we transmit a one-dimensional fairy tale through our schools and public discourse. Who would deny that the founders were brave, wise men whose pledge of "our lives, our fortunes, and our sacred honor" on behalf of the new United States was a heroic act? (This was no mere rhetoric; many signers of the Declaration of Independence lost their lives, fortunes, or both.) Daring yet practical dreamers, they combined free-thinking creativity with a shrewd understanding of human nature. A hundred years before he uttered it, they grasped the eternal truth of Lord Acton's admonition that "power tends to corrupt and absolute power corrupts absolutely." Their great achievement was to devise or refine principles and mechanisms—including checks and balances among separate branches of government, separation of church and state, and a Bill of Rights limiting government's power over citizens—that would protect against the incursions on freedom that human nature (inevitably?) would lead government officials to attempt. The founders were giants among men. But men they were, susceptible to the self-interest and historical limits of any mortal, so it's not surprising that the system of government they created initially limited freedom and democracy to people like themselves: male, white, and well-off. Those limits, and the resistance they provoked from the excluded, have reverberated through American history ever since.

The entire saga is foreshadowed in those five revolutionary words "all men are created equal." Inclusive as this phrase doubtless sounded to eighteenth-century ears, it left out half the population. Women had no right to vote, and did not gain it nationally until another 150 years had passed. Nor were "all men" welcome in the new democracy. Though the phrase made no mention of skin color (a fact civil rights activists would later turn to their advantage), in practice political rights were violently withheld from both the black men who were brought to the continent as slaves and the red men who were its original inhabitants. Indeed, the Constitution defined blacks as three-fifths of a person for census purposes (a device insisted upon by Southerners, for it boosted their representation in Congress). And there was the final limit of class, then as now the true unmentionable in American discourse. At a time when only 3 percent of the population owned much property, one had to be wealthy to be eligible for public office. (Benjamin Franklin and Thomas Paine advocated universal male suffrage but lost out to John Adams and Alexander Hamilton, who argued, "Those who own this country ought to govern it.")

The conventional version of United States history leaves Americans barely aware of these and other disquieting aspects of our past. Every schoolchild hears about Patrick Henry's ringing assertion, "Give me liberty or give me death!" but few learn that Henry was also a slave owner, as were almost half the signers of the Declaration of Independence. James W. Loewen, a scholar at the Smithsonian Institution in Washington, analyzed twelve of the American history textbooks most widely used in high schools in the United States for his illuminating 1995 book *Lies My Teacher Told Me*. Only two of the twelve texts even mention Henry's ownership of slaves. Only six note that Thomas Jefferson owned slaves. Owning slaves does not invalidate Jefferson's other contributions to American democracy, but it does suggest how deeply the scourge of racism is embedded in the national psyche. If it infected even our greatest visionary, how could it fail to leave an imprint on the larger nation?

The civil rights breakthroughs of the 1960s led to a more honest portrayal of the miseries blacks suffered under slavery, but textbooks still treated slavery as something that happened almost by itself; the role of whites remained obscured. Although lynchings were common in the South through the 1920s, not one of the textbooks included a photograph of a lynching. When Loewen tried to include one in a textbook he wrote, the book was rejected by inspectors for Mississippi. In the ensuing court case, one inspector agreed that lynchings had taken place but argued that there was no point in dwelling on such unpleasantness; it had all happened so long ago. "It is a history book, isn't it?" asked the judge, who ruled in the book's favor.

The true history of relations with Native Americans is equally unknown. The version taught to schoolchildren goes something like this: The Pilgrims found a land sparsely inhabited by primitive but friendly savages who taught them how to fish and plant corn. The grateful Pilgrims invited the Indians to a Thanksgiving feast (still the most American holiday). Whites tried to civilize the Indians, but Indians wouldn't adopt a modern way of life. They began attacking whites; scalping was a favorite tactic. Whites fought back, and with help from the United States cavalry settled the West. George Custer was defeated at Little Bighorn, but eventually the Indians were overcome. They were given land on reservations, victims of nothing more than the march of progress that is synonymous with American history.

A more realistic view was offered by Philip Sheridan, a

nineteenth-century army general who became famous for saying, "The only good Indian is a dead Indian." The reason Indians fought whites, Sheridan wrote, was that "we took away their country and their means of support. . . . Could anyone expect less?" Occasionally whites tried to legitimize such thefts through negotiated agreements. The federal government passed the Indian Removal Act of 1830, promising tribes new lands to the west in exchange for whites' taking over desirable lands in the Southeast. But the states of Alabama, Mississippi, and Georgia simply seized the land they wanted without paying. The tribes complained that this violated their treaties with Washington; the Supreme Court agreed. But President Andrew Jackson ignored the Court, then had the nerve to urge the tribes to sign new treaties to remove them even farther west. In 1869 a commission appointed by President Ulysses S. Grant admitted that "the history of the Government connections with the Indians is a shameful record of broken treaties and unfulfilled promises . . . murder, outrage, robbery, and wrongs."

A great irony lurks behind these transgressions, for the founding ideals and institutions of American democracy may have derived in part from Native American sources. In 1754, when Benjamin Franklin was trying to convince colonial leaders to unite against British domination, he invoked the example of the Iroquois League, a long-standing, democratically run alliance of six Iroquois nations. Our history books note the founders' philosophical debts to the ancient Greeks and to such European thinkers as Locke and Rousseau, but Iroquois influences go unmentioned, though they are plainly visible in the Articles of Confederation and the Constitution—especially in the concepts of states' rights and the separation of powers.

FREEDOM MUST BE FOUGHT FOR

Race is America's enduring dilemma but also its redemptive glory. It was, after all, descendants of slaves who brought forth jazz, arguably America's single greatest contribution to world art. Although developed by musicians of all races, jazz has always been dominated by blacks, those Americans who, as Ken Burns and Geoffrey C. Ward put it in their film and accompanying book *Jazz*, "had the peculiar experience of being unfree in a free land." Jazz beautifully expresses the dialectic between hope and despair that has forever animated America's struggle over race; it also embodies the tension between individual freedom and the common good that is the essence of democratic citizenship. As critic Charles S. Johnson marveled in 1925, "What an immense, even if unconscious, irony the Negroes have devised! They, who of all Americans are . . . least considered and most denied, have forged the key to the interpretation of the American spirit."

Few nations boast the racial diversity found in the United States; we are truly a rainbow nation. According to the 2000 census, America is still a majority (72 percent) white nation, but not for long. By 2050 the United States is expected to look like today's California, where whites make up just under 50 percent of the population and the rapidly growing Hispanic population makes Spanish the first language in many neighborhoods.

Yet racial discrimination clearly persists. Racial profiling leads police to stop black automobile drivers far more frequently than whites. The National Academy of Science's Institute of Medicine has documented that blacks and other minorities receive lower-quality health care than whites, even after correcting for differences in income and insurance coverage. Blacks and Hispanics are imprisoned, and sent to death row, at much higher rates than their population size would suggest. And Americans of all races still find it next to impossible to talk honestly across racial lines about what race means.

We find racial progress elusive, I believe, partly because we have avoided a full acknowledgment of our past. As a character in William Faulkner's *Requiem for a Nun* observed, "The past is never dead. It's not even past." History is all around us, and we cannot escape its legacy without first confronting it. The starkest example is the least mentioned. Never has our nation faced up to the original sin of its founding—the wholesale murder of Native Americans and the theft of their lands. At this late date, it is unrealistic to make full amends, but surely the descendants of America's original inhabitants deserve better than segregation on "reservations" where the only economic opportunities are mining, which pollutes their lungs and land, or gambling, which fuels the alcoholism that has punished them so terribly in the past.

Why could we not at least issue a formal apology, a statement of regret by the federal government, acknowledging the past and apologizing for the suffering imposed on Native Americans? Washington did this for Japanese-Americans who were confined during World War II; it even paid internees up to twenty thousand dollars each in reparations. That precedent has been invoked by Representative John Conyers and other leading African-Americans who are mounting an increasingly visible campaign seeking reparations for slavery.

There is no sign Congress will take up these issues anytime soon, and it is clear that, as with Native Americans, full repayment for the wealth stolen under slavery would be financially impractical; the bill, even excluding interest, would run into hundreds of billions of dollars. But in these matters, the exact dollar amount is not the point; public acknowledgment of past injustice is.

Truth and reconciliation commissions in South Africa, Argentina, and other nations have demonstrated that confronting past injustice is difficult and painful; nevertheless, it helps to purge the resentments that otherwise keep people from transcending the past. The United States, too, would be healthier if we expanded our vision to include the totality of our history—the dark, bright, and in-between—and admitted that race remains a huge, generally unspoken divide in our country. Most whites seem to believe that race is no longer a problem in the United States; most blacks believe it has always been one.

I write these words on the birthday of Martin Luther King Jr., now a national holiday. Among the politicians attending ceremonies in honor of the late civil rights leader today was President Bush, who praised King for refusing to "answer hatred with hatred, or meet violence with violence." It was an odd choice of words for a man who had just ordered three months of bombing in Afghanistan to retaliate for the September 11 attacks, but no odder than Bush's daring to bask in King's glory in the first place. Less than two years before, Bush had not hesitated to betray King's legacy to salvage his own presidential campaign. Faltering beneath an unexpectedly strong challenge from Senator John McCain, Bush faced a do-or-die primary vote in South Carolina, where tension ran high over whether the Confederate flag should continue to fly above the state capitol. Despite many opportunities, Bush refused to condemn display of this symbol of slavery. His appeal to racist sensibilities helped defeat McCain.

The contrast between King and Bush reveals the same dynamic that pervades much of American history: a struggle between the glorious promise of "liberty and justice for all," to quote the Pledge of Allegiance our schoolchildren recite, and the realities of privilege and hypocrisy that obstruct that promise. The struggle has ebbed and flowed, but overall our history supports King's faith that "the arc of the moral universe is long, but it bends towards justice." Not without a fight, though. "Power concedes nothing without a demand," as abolitionist Frederick Douglass famously pointed out. But Douglass, King, and other American insurgents had a crucial advantage: the ideals they advocated were, in theory, the law of the land. For all their personal inconsistencies, the founders left behind a framework guaranteeing citizens unprecedented rights and freedoms. It remained for citizens to invoke those rights, fight for them, and make them reality.

Some of the most inspiring pages in the history of American freedom were written by the civil rights movement of the 1950s and 1960s. Displaying immense bravery and determination, thousands upon thousands of average citizens, including a minority of whites, organized boycotts, sit-ins, prayer meetings, marches, and other protests that ended up changing the country forever. Government authorities were indifferent at best to the movement's calls for protection from the violence directed at them by local police and racists, yet the movement maintained its courage and direction, achieving victories of fundamental importance, including the Civil Rights Act of 1964 and the Voting Rights Act of 1965. Terror and bloodshed continued, King himself was assassinated, but by the end of the 1960s the United States had been irreversibly transformed. The civil rights movement had forced the country to live up to its founding principles. The movement had not only improved blacks' self-esteem and living conditions, it had raised up the entire nation and demonstrated to the world at large America's enviable capacity for self-correction.

The fight for freedom is contagious. The civil rights movement helped galvanize the women's liberation movement that emerged in the 1960s, just as the abolitionist movement of the nineteenth century had sparked an earlier wave of feminist organizing. In 1840 Elizabeth Cady Stanton traveled to England with her husband to attend an anti-slavery meeting. When the meeting refused to allow Stanton and other women to participate, a light went off in her head. How was sexual inequality any more defensible than racial inequality? At the time, American women could not vote, own property, enter college, or serve in the ministry, law, or other professions. Stanton came home and convened what Howard Zinn in *A People's History of the United States* calls "the first Women's Rights Convention in history." The convention produced a manifesto that mimicked the Declaration of Independence but with key changes: "We hold these truths to be self-evident: that all men and women are created equal . . ."

Women's suffrage did not become law for another fifty years (the arc of the moral universe is long), and despite the feminist movement of the 1970s, women in the United States today still do not enjoy economic parity with men. But the so-called second wave of feminism did revolutionize America's consciousness about the roles and rights of women, liberating males and females alike from old prejudices about women's supposed inferiority and empowering women to demand access to jobs and lifestyles that would have been inconceivable to their mothers' generation. As Susan Faludi relates in *Backlash*, this assertion of freedom soon was met by a counter-reaction from traditionalists who preferred women to remain dutiful wives and mothers. The fight still rages, and the battle over abortion in particular remains contentious, but some changes seem irreversible. Even young women who decline to call themselves feminists take it for granted that they can pursue careers, delay marriage or shun it altogether, and in general live for themselves rather than solely through a husband or children. Full equality remains elusive, but spend some time abroad and it's clear that American women enjoy more economic, political, and personal freedom than women anywhere on earth except northern Europe. (What American mother wouldn't envy her Dutch counterpart? Mothers in Holland enjoy three months' paid maternity leave and guaranteed return to their jobs.)

"No, I don't want my daughter to work," said Mustafa, a twenty-eight-year-old social worker and widower who shared a cup of tea with me in the ancient Egyptian city of Luxor, on the river Nile, while his mother-in-law watched his four-year-old. "School, yes, I want her to go to school, but then she must marry and have children." I was surprised. Arab culture is patriarchal—often the only people I saw waiting on platforms at train stations were men and boys—but Mustafa seemed a pretty Western guy. He spoke good English, had an advanced degree, loved watching American movies and television shows. I asked why he didn't want his daughter to work. "If she works, there will be men at her job looking at her, talking to her." And the problem with that? "Men cannot talk to her," he replied sharply. "It is forbidden."

"Japan is my home, but I feel less free here," Hitomi, a wife and mother who lives in Yokosuka, told me in Japan. After living in California for nearly seven years, Hitomi had returned to Japan four years earlier; she had a three-year-old son and a second child due any day. Over lunch one afternoon she said, "There are many rules and customs here, unwritten ones but important to follow." I reached to pour myself another cup of green tea. "For example," she said, "as the woman, I should be pouring your tea. Instead of just enjoying my meal, I should be thinking about you, whether you might want something to drink, are you enjoying your lunch." Such deference reflects the male dominance enshrined in Japanese culture centuries ago, and it shows few signs of weakening. Even now, Hitomi said, it's difficult for Japanese women who become mothers to continue working; their proper work is thought to be at home, raising children.

It's easy for Americans to forget: we live in a land of freedom, but many people in the world do not. That makes our nation a symbol to the world, which in turn confers certain responsibilities on us. If we want to be admired as the epitome of freedom, we must live up to that vision. The achievements of the women's and civil rights movements illustrate a central lesson of American history: freedom is never mere words on a page, no matter how eloquently stated. Freedom must be demanded, fought for, earned. And then it must be defended. That lesson needs emphasizing today, when American freedom is under assault both from without and from within. In times of war, it is common for the authorities to urge restrictions on civil liberties, due process, and other cornerstones of freedom. It is the duty of a free people to scrutinize such proposals and, where necessary, resist or modify them. The unruffled response the Bush administration's assault on liberty has received suggests that many Americans do take our freedoms for granted. Which is an excellent way to end up losing them, and the world's admiration as well.

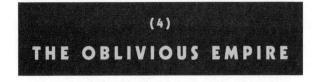

(4)
THE OBLIVIOUS EMPIRE

Texans are the worst," said the London cabbie. It was a fine late summer morning and we were waiting for the light to change so we could cross the Thames. "I had one in the cab a few weeks ago, must have been in his thirties. We were driving past the London Eye and he says, 'What's 'at?' I tell him it's the London Eye, the tallest Ferris wheel in the world. He says, 'We got one bigger than that.' I thought, 'Uh-oh, one of those.' I mean, I don't care if the Eye is the tallest in the world or not, maybe there is a bigger one in Texas for all I know. It's the bragging and the arrogance that put me off. No matter what he saw, Texas had more. I forget what we passed next, a double-decker bus, maybe, or Big Ben—something totally unique to London. He says, 'What's 'at?' I tell him. He says, 'We got one bigger than that.' After that I couldn't be bothered."

The light went green, the cabbie hit the accelerator. "I like most Americans," he added, "but it is quite amazing how they don't know anything about other places in the world"—he shot me a sly glance through the rearview mirror—"unless they're invading them."

The cabbie delivered that little jab on September 10, 2001, but I doubt he would have repeated it two days later. In the immediate aftermath of September 11, the mood in Europe was one of shock and deep sympathy for Americans. "We are very sorry," friends in Paris told me, as if I myself had been attacked. A couple of days later, in Prague, I happened to walk by the United States embassy one night on the way to dinner. The entire block was softly lit by candles well-wishers had left, along with hundreds of flowers and notes of condolence and encouragement. I found more flowers and notes at one of Prague's most revered public places: the monument on Wenceslas Square where the student Jan Palach set himself on fire to protest the Soviet crackdown of 1968. "No Terrorism" read one message spray-painted onto the concrete. Newspapers across the Continent ran articles reporting similar acts of solidarity in Japan, Russia, and elsewhere, as well as commentaries declaring, "We are all Americans now."

The sympathy was genuine and genuinely touching, but as I continued in the following weeks to talk with people across Europe and to survey the local media, it was also clear that the terror attacks had not caused Europeans to forget whatever they had once believed about the United States. Good manners might have restrained the London cabbie from repeating his remark, but it didn't mean he'd stopped thinking Americans were arrogant know-nothings. History did not begin on September 11.

Horrified as they were by the tragedy in the United States, many foreigners were not exactly surprised. Most of them knew the reasons why the United States was resented, even hated, in parts of the world, and they usually had complaints of their own. A high school teacher in Spain offered condolences for the September 11 victims and their families, but he told me he hoped Americans would recognize that the tragedy was "a consequence of U.S. foreign policy," especially its one-sided approach to the Israeli-Palestinian conflict. Some Europeans went so far as to cite America's conduct overseas as a virtual justification for the attacks. Even those who rejected the argument that the United States had brought September 11 on itself admitted that America could be infuriating at times.

Perhaps nothing irritates foreigners more than America's habit of thinking it has all the answers, and the right to impose them on everyone else. An outstanding example was President Bush's first major speech after the terror attacks. Speaking before Congress on September 20, Bush declared that foreign nations had to understand that, in the impending U.S.-led war against terrorism, "either you are with us, or you are with the terrorists." Like Bush's declaration that he wanted bin Laden "dead or alive," this was more cowboy talk, the Wild West sheriff warning, "Do as I say or get out of town"—the very attitude that had irritated America's friends and enemies alike for decades. Never mind that many nations already had their own painful experiences with terrorism; they would follow Washington's orders or else.

The United States would never accept such ultimatums itself, yet the arrogance of Bush's remark went unnoticed by America's political and journalistic elite. The *International Herald Tribune*, the overseas daily published by the *New York Times* and the *Washington Post*, did not even mention Bush's statement until the twentieth paragraph of its story, deep inside the paper. By contrast, the French daily *Le Monde* highlighted it three times on its front page, including in the headline and first paragraph. If opinion polls can be trusted, ordinary Americans also saw nothing wrong with their president's stance toward the rest of the world. Throughout the autumn of 2001, Bush's approval rating remained at above 75 percent.

But I would plead ignorance rather than venality on behalf of my fellow Americans. The embarrassing truth is that most of us know little about the outside world, and we are particularly ill-informed about what our government is doing in our name overseas. For example, Americans are ceaselessly, and accurately, reminded that Saddam Hussein is an evil man, but not that American-enforced economic sanctions have, since 1991, caused the deaths of at least 350,000 Iraqi children and impoverished a once prosperous Iraqi middle class. The bloody violence between Israelis and Palestinians that raged throughout March and April of 2002 got plenty of media coverage in the United States. Nevertheless, many Americans remained uninformed about basic aspects of the conflict. A poll conducted in early May by the University of Maryland's Program on International Policy Attitudes revealed, for example, that only 32 percent of Americans were aware that more Palestinians than Israelis had died in the fighting; only 43 percent knew that most other countries in the world disapproved of America's Middle East policies; and a mere 27 percent knew that most countries were more sympathetic to the Palestinian than to the Israeli side of the dispute.

In the wake of September 11, the question obsessing Americans about the Muslim world was "Why do they hate us?" But Muslims had long wondered the same about Americans. In a sparkling exception to most American news coverage, Sandy Tolan reported on National Public Radio in January 2002 that nearly everyone he had interviewed during six weeks of recent travel through the Middle East resented the negative stereotypes attached to Muslims and Arabs by

American movies, television, and news coverage. In Europe, stretching back to the novels of Goethe and the operas of Mozart, there had long been respect for the great achievements of Islamic civilization in culture, astronomy, architecture, and more. America, by contrast, regarded Muslims as primitive, untrustworthy fanatics, worth dealing with only because they had oil.

"You are dealing here with people who are almost childlike in their understanding of what is going on in the world," Gerald Celente, director of the Trends Research Institute in Rhinebeck, New York, told the *Financial Times* shortly after September 11. "It's all: 'We never did anything to anybody, so why are they doing this to us?' "

Some Americans have taken refuge in the obvious answer: they envy our wealth and resent our power. There is truth in this, as I'll discuss, but it barely scratches the surface. The reason many foreigners don't share Americans' high opinion of themselves is simple: they dislike both how America behaves overseas and its attitude about that behavior.

America, foreigners say, is a trigger-happy bully that is both out for itself and full of itself. It feels no obligation to obey international law; it often pushes other countries around, forcing on them policies and sometimes tyrannical leaders that serve only American interests, and then, if they resist too much, it may bomb obedience into them with cruise missiles. Only an American would blink to hear the United States called the most bellicose major power in the world; to foreigners, the observation is obvious to the point of banality. America's high-handed behavior puzzles admirers of its domestic freedoms: how to explain the inconsistency? Less sentimental observers point out that this is how the strong have treated the weak throughout history. But, they add, what makes the

United States uniquely annoying is its self-righteous insistence that it does nothing of the kind, that it is the epitome of evenhanded virtue and selfless generosity—the Beacon of Democracy that other nations should thank and emulate.

On November 10, 2001, President Bush made his first appearance before the United Nations General Assembly and, in a speech praised by the *New York Times* for its "plain-spoken eloquence," told the rest of the world it wasn't doing enough to help the United States fight terrorism. "Every nation in the world has a stake in this cause," declared Bush before lecturing his audience that the responsibility to fight terrorism was "binding on every nation with a place in this chamber." Yet on the same day—indeed, at the very moment—that Bush was admonishing others about their international responsibilities, his own administration was shunning negotiations in Morocco to finalize the Kyoto protocol on global warming. Talk about an issue that every nation has a stake in! Already the earth's glaciers are melting, sea levels are rising, and catastrophic storms are becoming more severe and frequent—this after a mere 1 degree Fahrenheit increase in temperatures over the past century. The scientific consensus predicts 3 to 10.5 degrees of additional warming by 2100, bringing more violent weather, flooded coastlines, and social havoc. Yet the Bush administration insists on doing nothing to lower U.S. greenhouse gas emissions. No wonder foreigners resent us.

American elites sometimes talk of our nation's isolationist tendencies, but the correct adjective is unilateralist. The United States has hardly shunned overseas involvement over the years; we simply insist on setting our own terms. This tendency has become especially pronounced since victory in the Cold War left us the only remaining superpower. Determined

to keep it that way, senior officials in the first Bush administration drafted a grand strategy for the new era (which got
leaked to the *New York Times*): henceforth the goal of American foreign policy would be to prevent any other nation or alliance from becoming a superpower; the United States would
rule supreme. This strategy lives on under George W. Bush—
which is no surprise, since Vice President Dick Cheney and
other key advisers were the ones who devised the strategy for
Bush's father. Shortly after taking office, the administration of
Bush II announced it was going to withdraw from the Anti-
Ballistic Missile Treaty, a cornerstone of nuclear arms control
for the past thirty years, in an assertion of unilateralism that
evoked dismay not just from treaty partner Russia but from
the entire global community. Bush's oddest rejection of global
cooperation was his refusal to join, even retroactively, the
accord against bioterrorism reached in July 2001 that could
hinder future anthrax attacks. The United States delegation
walked out of the negotiations because the Bush administration refused to accept the same rules it demands for Iraq and
other "rogue states": international inspections of potential
weapons production sites.

I don't mean to pick on Mr. Bush. Double standards have
a long bipartisan pedigree in American foreign policy. Bush's
father uttered one of the most feverish declarations of American prerogative in 1988, while serving as Ronald Reagan's
vice president. Five years earlier, when the Soviet Union shot
down a Korean Airlines passenger jet over the Pacific, killing
all 276 people on board, the United States had condemned
the attack as further evidence of the "evil empire's" true nature, rejecting the Soviet explanation that the jet was acting
like a military aircraft. Now the tables were turned: the
United States had shot down an Iranian civilian jet it mistak-

enly believed was a military craft. All 290 passengers died. When Bush senior was asked if an apology was in order, he replied, "I will never apologize for the United States. I don't care what the facts are."

Democrats have been just as bad about this kind of thing. In 1998 critics at home and abroad were condemning the Clinton administration's launch of cruise missiles against Iraq as at best unnecessary and at worst a self-serving ploy to weaken impeachment proceedings against the president. But no, Secretary of State Madeleine Albright modestly explained, "if we have to use force, it is because we are America. We are the indispensable nation. . . . We see farther into the future." As Rupert Cornwell, the Washington correspondent for the British newspaper *The Independent*, observed on another occasion, "No one wraps self-interest in moral superiority quite like the Americans do."

Americans are a fair-minded people, however, and I doubt that a majority of us would support such hypocrisy if we were truly aware of it. I believe most of us would instead urge that the United States bring its global behavior into accord with its domestic principles. But that might threaten what Washington considers vital national interests, so the powers that be resist. Since America is the land of both Hollywood and Madison Avenue, our official response has instead been to hire public relations experts to do a better job of "getting our message out" overseas. Brilliant touch, no? After all, the problem couldn't possibly be our policies themselves.

Americans will continue to misunderstand the world, and our place within it, until we face the full truth of how our government has acted overseas—a fact made powerfully clear to me in South Africa, where the enthusiasm for America shown by Malcolm Adams is balanced by the anger of those who recall that the United States was a firm, long-standing supporter of apartheid.

WHY DON'T THEY LOVE US?

The ferry from Cape Town takes forty minutes to reach Robben Island, the notorious prison where Nelson Mandela and other South African freedom fighters were jailed during their struggle for freedom. The ferry lands at a jetty two hundred yards from a complex of low buildings with corrugated tin roofs that is the prison proper. A sign retained from apartheid days reads, in English and Afrikaans, "Robben Island. Welcome. We Serve with Pride."

There are now guided tours of the island, and what makes them especially compelling is that they are conducted by the former prisoners themselves. My group was greeted by a thin man in a white windbreaker named Siphiwo Sobuwa. Speaking in a flat, deliberate tone, Sobuwa said he had been imprisoned at age seventeen after being captured smuggling arms for the ANC's military wing. Interrogated, beaten, denied a lawyer, he was sentenced to forty-eight years in jail. He served fifteen years, all on Robben Island, before the crumbling of apartheid enabled his release in 1991.

As he ushered us into the prison's entry hall, Sobuwa recalled how he spent his first two years in solitary confinement because he didn't speak Afrikaans. A warden told his group of arriving prisoners that no talking was allowed, but since Sobuwa didn't understand Afrikaans, he asked another inmate what was going on. The warden decided to make an example of Sobuwa. "I was sent to A section, the torture section," he told us. "I could not write or receive letters. I could not speak, sing, or whistle. Food was slipped underneath the grille of my cell. Those two years were the hardest."

We pushed through a door into an open-air courtyard, where we listened to Sobuwa recount other punishments common on Robben Island. Most humiliating was the guards' game of ordering an inmate buried in the ground up to his neck and then leaving him there all day to roast in the sun while guards took turns urinating on him. More gruesome was the practice of hanging a prisoner upside down from a tree and waiting as the hours passed for him to pass out and, in one case, to perish as the body's blood supply gradually accumulated in the brain, starving it of oxygen. But of all the deprivations—punishing physical labor, numbing boredom, inedible food, lack of heat—Sobuwa said the blackout on news was the hardest to bear. Inmates did their best to compensate. "The guard towers had no toilets," he explained, "so guards would relieve themselves in newspapers, then throw the papers down to the ground. We would retrieve those papers, scrape them off, and read the news they contained. We didn't care what kind of mess was inside, we wanted that news."

Hearing about such abominations firsthand makes visiting Robben Island as unforgettable as a pilgrimage to Dachau or Hiroshima. And talking with a man like Sobuwa rescues foreign policy from its usual abstractions, making concrete the implications of such diplomatic double-talk as "constructive engagement," the Reagan administration's justification for its unswerving support for apartheid. When I interviewed Sobuwa at his cinder-block house in a Cape Town township, he said his work had taught him to distinguish between Americans as people and the American government. He had little good to say about the latter. Washington, he pointed out, as well as Israel, had supported apartheid—and thus the oppression on Robben Island—until the very end. Furthermore, he said, "it is a trend among United States presidents that so-called Third World countries must be destabilized. America believes in solving problems not by negotiations but through military pressure."

But his tour guide conversations had made Sobuwa realize that not all Americans supported their government's policy. He was grateful for those who had joined the protests that eventually forced Western governments, including that of the United States, to endorse apartheid's demise. He was unaware that America's new vice president had, as a U.S. congressman in 1985, voted against urging Mandela's release from jail, but then neither were most Americans aware of this aspect of Dick Cheney's past. What Sobuwa did know was that Bill Clinton had a lot of nerve. "He came here a couple years ago to visit Mandela and speak to our Parliament, and he told us South Africa should cut its ties to Cuba because Cuba was a bad government. Well, when we needed help during our liberation struggle, Cuba gave it. When we needed food, Cuba provided it. For someone who did not help our struggle to come now and ask us to distance ourselves from someone who did, that is very arrogant behavior."

Arrogant but, alas, not atypical. The United States has long pressed South American nations to cut ties with the Castro government. Likewise, in June 2002 George W. Bush announced that Yasir Arafat had to go as the Palestinian leader. Free elections had to be held, said Bush, but Washington would push for a Palestinian state only if those "free" elections got rid of Arafat.

Washington's might-makes-right view of such matters was succinctly expressed by Henry Kissinger when, as President Richard Nixon's national security adviser, he privately defended overthrowing the elected government of Chile by say-ing he saw no reason why the United States had to allow Chile to "go Marxist" simply because "its people are irre-sponsible." Testifying before the U.S. Senate on the day of the coup, Kissinger claimed the United States had played no role in the 1973 coup that toppled Allende. But voluminous government documents show that Kissinger, as head of the so-called Forty Committee that supervised U.S. covert actions between 1969 and 1976, was well-informed about how the CIA had ordered a coup in 1970 that had failed to thwart Al-lende and, in 1973, had at least condoned if not actively aided the Chilean military men who, under future dictator General Augusto Pinochet, imposed martial law and eventually killed 3,197 Chilean citizens.

Note the date of the U.S.-sponsored assault on democratic government in Chile: September 11, 1973. Note the esti-mated Chilean death toll—executions plus military casual-ties—of 3,197 people. Is not the congruence between that coup and the World Trade Center attack striking? True, one was authored by religious fanatics and the other by a state, and the events were separated in time by twenty-eight years, yet both took place on the same date and caused compar-able numbers of deaths. Nevertheless, this eerie coincidence passed virtually unremarked in the United States.

This is self-defeating. It's no secret to Chileans that the United States helped bring to power the dictatorship that ruled them for seventeen years. Nor are the people of El Sal-vador and Guatemala unaware that the United States gave money, weapons, and training to the military governments that killed so many of their fellow citizens in recent decades. In Guatemala, a truth commission sponsored by the United Nations concluded in 1999 that "American training of the officer corps in counterinsurgency techniques" was a "key factor" in a "genocide" that included the killing of 200,000 peasants.

Switch to Asia or the Middle East and the same point applies. Virtually every one of Washington's allies in the Middle East is an absolute monarchy where democracy and human rights are foreign concepts and women in particular are second-class citizens. But they have oil, so all is forgiven. Likewise, in South Korea everyone knows that the United States chose the generals that ruled their country from the end of World War II until 1993; the facts came out during a trial that found two of the surviving dictators guilty of state terrorism. Ferdinand Marcos of the Philippines, General Suharto of Indonesia, General Lon Nol of Cambodia—the list of tyrants that Washington has supported in Asia is widely known, except in the United States.

Again, what offends is not simply the ruthlessness of American policies but their hypocrisy. The United States insists on the sanctity of United Nations resolutions when they punish enemies like Iraq with arms inspections, but not when they oblige its number-one foreign aid recipient, Israel, to withdraw from occupation of Palestinian territories in the West Bank and Gaza. On trade policy, Washington demands that poor countries honor World Trade Organization rules against subsidizing domestic farmers or industries because these rules enable U.S.-based multinational firms to invade those countries' economies. Without blushing, Washington then lavishes billions of dollars in subsidies on our own agriculture sector (dominated, by the way, by those same multinationals) and imposes tariffs against foreign steel imports. Why do we violate fair play so brazenly? Because we can. "The United States can hurt us a lot worse than we can hurt them," grumbled one Canadian trade official.

Then there is our self-serving definition of "terrorism," a concept America's political and media elites never apply to the United States or its allies, only to enemies or third parties. No one disputes that the September 11 attacks against the United States were acts of terrorism; that is, they targeted innocent civilians to advance a political or military agenda. When the Irish Republican Army exploded bombs inside London subway stations and department stores in the mid-1990s, that, too, was terrorism. So were the Palestinian suicide bombings in Israel in early 2002, and Saddam Hussein's use of poison gas against Kurds in Iraq in 1988. But when Israel attacked Palestinian refugee camps in April 2002, demolishing buildings and killing or wounding many civilians, was that not also terrorism? When the United States lobbed Volkswagen-sized shells into Lebanese villages in 1983 and dropped "smart bombs" on Baghdad in 1991, many innocent civilians perished while Washington sent its geopolitical message. The napalm dropped during the Vietnam War, the bombing of Dresden, and the annihilation of Hiroshima and Nagasaki in World War II—these acts all pursued military or political objectives by killing vast numbers of civilians, just as the September 11 attacks did. Yet in mainstream American discourse, the United States is never the perpetrator of terrorism, only its victim and implacable foe.

These and other unsavory aspects of America's overseas dealings are not completely unknown in the United States. Academic specialists, human rights activists, and partisans of the political left are familiar with this history. Glimpses of the truth appear (very) occasionally in mainstream press coverage, and the CIA's role in subverting democracies and overthrowing governments was documented by congressional investigations in 1975. In 2002 Samantha Powers published a book,

A Problem from Hell, that meticulously documented how Washington deliberately chose not to intervene against some of the worst acts of genocide in the twentieth century, including Pol Pot's rampages in Cambodia, ethnic cleansing in Bosnia, and tribal slaughter in Rwanda. The book received considerable attention within media circles; its message got out. But in general, critical perspectives on American actions are given nowhere near the same prominence or repetition in government, media, and public discussion as is the conventional view of the United States as an evenhanded champion of democracy and freedom. Thus the basic direction of American foreign policy rarely shifts, and Washington creates for itself what the late *Wall Street Journal* reporter Jonathan Kwitny called "endless enemies" around the world. Worse, average Americans are left unaware that this is happening, and so are shocked when foreigners don't love us as much as we think they should.

Ignorance is an excuse, but it is no shield. "Although most Americans may be largely ignorant of what was, and still is, being done in their names, all are likely to pay a steep price . . . for their nation's continued efforts to dominate the global scene," veteran Asian affairs analyst Chalmers Johnson wrote in his fierce book, *Blowback*. America's tendency to bully, warns Johnson, will "build up reservoirs of resentment against all Americans—tourists, students, and businessmen, as well as members of the armed forces—that can have lethal results."

"Blowback" is a CIA term for how foreign policy can come back to haunt a country years later in unforeseen ways, especially after cases of secret operations. Thus Johnson quotes a 1997 report by the Pentagon's Defense Science Board: "Historical data show a strong correlation between U.S. involvement in international situations and an increase in terrorist attacks against the United States." A glaring example is the Iranian hostage crisis of 1979. To protect American oil interests, the CIA in 1953 overthrew the elected government of Iran and installed Shah Reza Pahlavi (an act a subsequent CIA director, William Colby, described as the CIA's "proudest moment"). The shah ruled with an iron hand, murdered thousands, duly became widely hated, and was forced from power in 1979. Residual Iranian anger led to an attack on the United States embassy in Tehran and seizure of fifty-four hostages, a crisis that doomed Jimmy Carter's presidency.

Because Johnson's book was published in 2000, it was unable to address the most spectacular of all cases of blowback: the September 11 terror attacks. But in the October 15 and December 10, 2001, issues of *The Nation*, Johnson explained how the CIA supported Osama bin Laden from at least 1984 as part of its funding of the mujahideen, the Islamic resistance to the Soviet Union's occupation of Afghanistan. The CIA funneled its support for bin Laden and other mujahideen, including building the complex where bin Laden trained some thirty-five thousand followers, through Pakistan's intelligence service. But bin Laden turned against the United States after the 1991 Persian Gulf War, when "infidel" American troops were stationed on the Islamic holy ground of Saudi Arabia to prop up its authoritarian regime. The September 11 attacks, Johnson concludes, were the blowback from America's covert action in Afghanistan in the 1970s, and the cycle is probably not over: "The Pentagon's current response of 'bouncing the rubble' in Afghanistan [is] setting the stage for more rounds to come."

Does that necessarily discredit the U.S. war in Afghanistan? After all, it did destroy or at least disperse much of bin Laden's al-Qaida network, liberate the country from the medieval clutches of the Taliban, and allow rebuilding to begin. The costs, however, were high. The exact number of civilian casualties remains uncertain but seems likely to exceed the approximately three thousand deaths that occurred in the September 11 attacks that motivated the war. Additional Afghans died from the preexisting famine, which the bombing prevented relief agencies from treating. "The whole Muslim world is watching this with shock and horror," a Saudi Arabian analyst told the *New York Times*. "Among the young, new animosities are created and there are new calls for revenge. This is dangerous; this is the atmosphere that creates terrorism."

DOING THE RIGHT THING

America is modest about very little, but it is curiously reticent about its status as the mightiest empire in history. Whereas previous empires gloried in their privileged status (Rome) or wrestled with its moral implications (Great Britain), the American empire simply tells itself it doesn't exist. By any historical definition, the United States is an empire of extraordinary power, but only in the wake of September 11 have even its elites begun using this term, and always favorably. Americans believe they are wealthy because they're decent, hardworking people (which they generally are), without realizing the huge advantages that America's overseas power secures for them, starting with the cheap, abundant Middle East oil that fueled the American economy's remarkable growth over the past fifty years.

The United States has acted like an empire from the beginning, repeatedly using force to expand its territory. It started by pushing Native Americans off their land. In the War of 1812, it drove the British into Canada once and for all, a display of strength that convinced Spain to give up its claim to the Southwest. With the Monroe Doctrine of 1823, the United States declared unofficial control over the entire western hemisphere. In 1898 it expanded overseas, "liberating" Cuba and the Philippines from Spain but making them virtual American colonies; it also chose an "Open Door" strategy of relying on economic more than military strength to dominate overseas. The first half of the twentieth century included dozens of foreign interventions to ensure friendly governments and protect U.S. business interests, especially in Central America.

The American empire reached maturity after emerging from World War II as by far the strongest and richest world power. Military bases were established throughout Europe, Asia, and the Middle East. The rules of international trade and finance were favorably rewritten to encourage expansion of American companies overseas. During the subsequent Cold War, the Soviet empire challenged but never seriously threatened the supremacy of its American counterpart. Today, thirteen years after the fall of the Berlin Wall, the United States maintains nearly the same global posture it did during the Cold War: scores of overseas military bases; the world's highest volume of arms sales (90 percent to undemocratic or human-rights-abusing governments); and massive nuclear overkill (each of its twenty-two Trident submarines can reduce four hundred cities to radioactive dust, and the Tridents are but a small part of the total arsenal). In short, the American empire shows no signs of either shrinking or retreating.

Do foreigners resent all this power? Do they envy the economic advantages it confers on the United States? Do they compensate by making the United States a scapegoat for their own shortcomings? Of course they do; psychologists call this human nature.

"I was talking with a correspondent from [the Russian news agency] Tass a few weeks after the September 11 attacks," Loren Jenkins, the foreign editor for National Public Radio, told me. "He said, 'You know, during the Cold War, half the world could hate the Soviet Union and the other half could hate the United States. Your problem now is you're the only ones left to hate. Anyone anywhere who is unhappy with his life will blame the United States.' "

"Most French people like America and Americans, but they regard its foreign policy as imperialistic and resent its tendency toward unilateralism," Laurent Joffrin, the editor of the leading French newsweekly magazine *Le Nouvel Observateur* told me in Paris. One source of the resentment is jealousy arising from France's own imperial past, Joffrin added. "All French schoolchildren learn that France used to be one of the world's great powers. They also learn that America came to our rescue twice in the last century, during World War I and World War II. On the one hand, we are grateful for America's help. On the other hand, it makes us resentful. One prefers to be the savior, not the saved."

As Joffrin's comment suggests, empires are not automatically evil. True, America had its own reasons for "saving" Europe, not just during the wars but afterward; the Marshall Plan that got European economies back on their feet also created new markets for American firms and weakened the appeal of Europe's Communist parties. But so what? Motives do not trump deeds in the making of history, and there is no denying that the effect of American policy was a better life for Europeans of all classes. The record is more mixed in regard to postwar Japan; despite substantial American reconstruction aid and technology transfers, Japan's economy did not take off until it received a surge of Pentagon contracts for the war in Korea (including an order for jeeps that saved a little company called Toyota from imminent bankruptcy). But in Japan, too, the effect of American policy was to revive a vanquished foe and improve the lives of its people.

Nor have all of America's overseas military interventions been on the side of darkness. When the Serbian dictator Slobodan Milosevic was orchestrating the slaughter of countless innocents throughout the territory of the former Yugoslavia in the early 1990s, the powers of western Europe responded with little more than pious hand-wringing. The United States did not react as quickly as it might have either, but in the end it was American firepower that stopped Milosevic. When I was reporting in eastern Africa during my first trip around the world in 1991, I was proud to see that the United States ambassador was actively opposing the brutish behavior of Daniel arap Moi, the corrupt ruler of Kenya. In Moscow that year, I interviewed U.S. embassy officials who were focusing much-needed attention on the catastrophic damage that the Soviet regime had done to Russia's ecosystems and public health. In China a few years later, American policy was torn between pressing the government to respect human rights and subordinating such concerns to the goal of expanding corporate access to the Chinese market, but at least there was a fight over which policy to pursue. Passing through Zimbabwe in 2001, I found abundant evidence of the strong-arm tactics that President Robert Mugabe was employing to stifle free speech and seize farmers' lands improperly. When Mugabe, as widely expected, stole the 2002 election, the Bush administration rightly condemned the vote as neither free nor fair.

History offers more such examples, but the point is, there is more to American foreign policy than funding dictators and overthrowing democracies. At times, our conduct overseas does match our ideals; at times we do do the right thing. The reason American foreign policy is not monochromatic, I believe, is that our commitment to higher principles is not mere sham. Our history, our laws, our very conception of who we are, require us to take seriously our oft-invoked reverence for freedom, democracy, human rights, and justice. Of course, other goals compete in shaping foreign policy, and different presidents weigh them differently: securing access to markets and natural resources, fostering inviting investment climates, pursuing geopolitical influence. In any case, there is a battle among these interests—both in official Washington, where the policies are made, and in the country at large, where the public must ratify the policies, if only implicitly.

Just as civil rights activists cited the Constitution to demand justice for all Americans, so can foreign policy critics insist that Washington square its rhetorical support for human rights with its dealings with Saudi Arabia, Turkey, and China. Because of past pressure from activists, the State Department is required to issue an annual report on the human rights performance of every country in the world. When the 2002 report revealed that many of the Bush administration's closest allies in the war on terror were egregious human rights abusers, it gave American citizens, the media, and Congress an opening to demand greater consistency in American policy. It was public pressure that forced the United States to withdraw from Vietnam in the 1970s, and fear of public reaction that has made the Pentagon wary ever since of committing U.S. ground troops overseas. It was the demonstrations and letter writing of anti-apartheid activists that forced even the Reagan administration to tone down its support of the white regime in South Africa in the 1980s. Similar pressure in the 1990s highlighted American complicity with sweatshop operators and other examples of globalization run amok.

On those occasions when American foreign policy does champion values of democracy and fair play, there are few more powerful forces for good in the world. The tragedy is how infrequently this is the case. It's not too late for this to change; as noted, many currents influence the flow of American foreign policy. But improvement is unlikely until the American people pay more attention to what their government is actually doing around the world, and demand something better.

OUR PALACE COURT PRESS

I believe that Americans are basically decent people," said Denis Halliday, the former head of the United Nations' humanitarian aid program in Iraq. "If they understood that Iraq is not made up of twenty-two million Saddam Husseins but made up of twenty-two million people—of families, of children, of elderly parents, families with dreams and hopes and expectations for their children and themselves—they would be horrified to realize that the current killing of innocent Iraqi civilians by the U.S. Air Force . . . is being done in their name."

At the time Halliday was being interviewed, in March 2002, Vice President Cheney was touring Europe and the Middle East, trying to build support for the Bush administration's desire to oust Saddam. According to Halliday, the administration was flagrantly violating both international law and moral decency: first by maintaining economic sanctions that were punishing Iraq's general population, and second by bombing Iraq while patrolling the "no-fly zone" established after the Persian Gulf War of 1991. What Halliday wanted to know was, "Where are the American people? Why are they not controlling their government, which seems to be running amok?"

Many times I've heard foreigners complain that Americans think only about themselves. Especially in Europe but elsewhere as well, we are thought of as nice, friendly folks, but childishly unsophisticated about the outside world and selfishly unconcerned about America's role in it. "Many of us have American friends," Ana, an intellectual in Barcelona, told me a couple of weeks after September 11, "but we wish our American friends would *think* a little more about their government, because we have to live with America's politics, and that is often difficult, especially when war is in the air."

Would foreigners be more forgiving if they knew how little critical information Americans receive about our government's foreign policy? How can Americans be expected to form considered opinions about the "war on terrorism" when our news media report little but the government's version of the truth? Members of the media need to "watch what they say," White House press spokesman Ari Fleischer said shortly after the September 11 attacks. Fleischer need hardly have bothered with his warning; the American press proved an eager amplifier of the government's message. "George Bush is the president. . . . [If] he wants me to line up, just tell me where," said one of the nation's most influential journalists, *CBS Evening News* anchor Dan Rather.

The biggest political joke in America is that we have a liberal press. It's a joke taken seriously by a surprisingly large number of people, including the nation's sizable right-wing minority (approximately one of every four voters). Their purchases propelled a book reiterating the myth, Bernard Goldberg's *Bias*, to the top of America's best-seller lists in early

2002. The notion of a liberal press was injected into the national consciousness thirty years ago by Richard Nixon, who blamed the press for losing the Vietnam War and inflating what he dismissed as a "third-rate burglary" into the Watergate scandal. Ever since, the myth of the liberal press has served as a political weapon for conservative and right-wing forces eager to discourage critical coverage of government and corporate power. And journalists and their superiors have fallen for the trick. They are forever asking themselves if their coverage is too liberal, never if it is too conservative.

Understand: In America, "liberal" means "left-wing," with its connotations of anti-government, anti-corporate, anti-establishment. The reality of how America's newspapers, television, radio, Internet, and other mass media operate could hardly be more different.

Anti-government? Most of what the American press reports about the U.S. government is the government's side of the story. Check any newspaper, peruse any broadcast. You find statement after statement of what the president said today about subject X, what the defense secretary said about topic Y, how proposal Z was received by the Senate or House majority leader. Often there are disputes among these officials—conflict being a necessary ingredient of the news narrative—but the disputes tend to be incremental or tactical. There is precious little reporting that stands back from the insider debates of Washington, challenges their underlying premises, or offers a genuinely alternative analysis.

"What we do most of the time is, we really are a transmission belt," confessed the late James Reston, who served for decades as the *New York Times*'s man in Washington. Of course, it is important to report the government's side of any story. But if that is all, or nearly all, of the story, the resulting picture is inevitably misleading. What citizens end up being told is not so much a lie as it is woefully incomplete, which can amount to the same thing. For example, the press repeatedly reported the Bush administration's claim to be taking extraordinary measures to avoid civilian casualties during the war in Afghanistan. Only rarely and long after the fact did it present contrary information. Thus news coverage left the impression that few innocents were being killed, when in fact the death toll was probably higher than the number killed in the September 11 attacks.

We do not, thank God, have a state-owned or state-controlled press in the United States. We do have a state-friendly one. That is, our press supports the prevailing political system, its underlying assumptions and power relations, and the economic and foreign policies that flow from them. Rarely are these liberal.

Americans and foreigners alike, I've learned, find the idea of a state-friendly press in the United States hard to grasp. They see the freedoms that permeate American life and they assume that a robust, diverse exchange of political ideas and information is naturally part of the mix. After all, freedom of the press is written into the very first amendment of our Bill of Rights. Alas, in contemporary America, that freedom exists in theory more than it gets exercised in practice. "It's always amazed me about you guys," a British journalist once told me. "We do lots of investigative reporting in Britain, even though our libel laws are quite strict. You guys have all the freedom in the world and you don't use it."

The best line ever written about the press, at least by an American, was by A. J. Liebling: "Freedom of the press is guaranteed only to those who own one." Nowadays, ownership of the American press has been captured by a handful of gigantic transnational corporations who are the farthest thing imaginable from leftist troublemakers or even law-abiding liberals. Should it surprise anyone that the news they provide downplays unconventional viewpoints, tough criticism of corporate and government elites, and other information uncongenial to the established order?

Believing in diversity of opinion and the press's role as a check and balance on entrenched power, Liebling worried in the 1940s about media ownership becoming concentrated in fewer and fewer hands. That was back when most major American cities boasted at least a handful of competing newspapers. What would he think today, when most cities are one-paper monopolies and a mere ten corporations control more than 50 percent of the country's media outlets—newspapers, radio and television stations, magazines, books, music and movies, and the Internet. Among these corporations are General Electric ($129.9 billion in annual revenues), which owns three news networks and thirteen broadcast stations; Sony ($53.8 billion), the movie and music producer; AT&T ($66 billion), which is America's largest cable provider; AOL Time Warner ($36.2 billion in revenues in 2000), whose properties include CNN and its *Headline News*, and *Time*; the Walt Disney Company ($25.4 billion), which owns ABC television and radio networks and sixty broadcast stations; Bertelsmann ($16.5 billion), America's largest publisher of trade books; and News Corporation ($11.6 billion), which owns the Fox television network, twenty-six broadcast stations, and the *New York Post*.

How to square this lineup of transnational titans with the myth of a liberal press? Being some of the largest corporations in the world, they can hardly be anti-establishment; they are pillars of the establishment. Three of them—Sony, Bertelsmann, and NewsCorp—are foreign-owned, but as transnational companies their loyalties are to no one land but instead to profitable engagement in as many markets as possible, and no market is richer than the United States. In sum, the handful of global conglomerates that dominate America's media system have about as much interest in challenging the status quo in America as elephants have in challenging the status quo of the jungle.

Of course, to produce the news, corporations have to hire journalists. The myth of the liberal press identifies these hirelings as the problem, asserting that their biases distort the news. That may sound plausible until you remember that the journalists answer to superiors who answer to higher superiors, all of whom are paid to make sure that the company produces what its bosses want. "Earnings is [*sic*] what I'm judged on," said Leslie Moonves, the president of the CBS network, justifying his plans to cut news division staff even after the September 11 attacks. Corporate control is not total, of course; the fast pace of daily journalism makes it impractical to check every decision with one's bosses. But it is the bosses who decide which journalists are hired and promoted, and they naturally choose individuals whose judgments accord with their own.

(Which, paradoxically, hints at the one plausible aspect of the liberal-press myth. Conservatives complain most vociferously about the media's coverage of social issues: abortion, gun control, homosexuality, religion. A 1998 survey of Washington editors and reporters found that they were indeed more "liberal" than most Americans on such issues; they were pro-choice on abortion, tolerant of gays, supportive of gun control. But the journalists were more conservative than average Americans on economic issues; they favored pro-corporate positions on taxation, trade, and government spending. Such a split philosophy mirrors that of the journalists' corporate superiors, most of whom are moderate Republicans or centrist Democrats who are enthusiastically pro-business on economic and political matters but shrink back from the conservative agenda on social issues. News coverage that reflects this view of the world may anger conservatives, but it is liberal in only a very limited sense.)

A STENOGRAPHER TO POWER

Overt censorship is sometimes used to keep journalists in line, but more common is self-censorship by journalists themselves. The simple necessity of obeying one's boss results in news that generally reflects a corporate view of the world, including a faith that unfettered private enterprise is a blessing for workers and capitalists alike; that the United States government is a force for good in the world; that globalization protesters are violent anarchists; and that cheerful, endless shopping is every American's patriotic duty.

Other messages are less welcome, as I myself have learned firsthand. Some years ago, one of my bosses threatened to fire me after I broadcast a radio satire poking fun at NBC television and McDonald's for running a million-dollar-a-night lottery designed to make Americans consume more junk food and television. "I know it was funny, but you were criticizing the free enterprise system," he told me. "You can't do that." In 2001, when a major national magazine recruited me to investigate the incoming administration of George W. Bush, I reached the unsurprising conclusion that the lifelong oilman planned to weaken environmental regulation. The editors demanded three rewrites to tone down my story, finally spelling out their bottom line: "This story has to appeal to all of our readers, including drivers of the SUVs advertised in our pages."

I could cite numerous other stories that never ran because their criticisms of the established order were too pointed, or that never even got assigned in the first place, but my personal experiences only hint at the larger problem. When I was writing *On Bended Knee*, a book about news coverage of the Reagan presidency, reporters told me about many other examples of direct and indirect censorship.

To understand why Americans don't know their own foreign policy, consider the story of the *New York Times* reporter Raymond Bonner. In 1983 Bonner was removed as the paper's Central America reporter after his dispatches revealed that Washington was backing terrorism and repression, not democracy and human rights, in its backyard. His most explosive article detailed how the El Salvadoran military's elite Atlacatl Battalion had massacred hundreds of peasants, mainly women, children, and old people, in December 1981; the battalion was the first military unit trained by the U.S. advisers President Reagan had dispatched to resist what he warned was an imminent Communist takeover of El Salvador. Bonner's story ran in the *Times* on January 27, 1982, the very day the Reagan administration certified to Congress that its client regime was making a "significant effort to comply with internationally recognized human rights." Reagan officials, joined by the *Wall Street Journal* editorial page and other right-wing voices in the press, mounted a fierce campaign to portray Bonner as soft on Communism, and within six months he was removed from the beat. But it was his own superiors at the *Times* who pulled the trigger on Bonner. "I think the real problem was that my reporting didn't fit the tenor of the times, or of the *Times* under Abe Rosenthal," Bonner later told me. Rosenthal, the newspaper's executive editor, denied that his reassignment of Bonner was anything more than normal bureaucratic shuffling. Still, the coincidence of events is striking. Because Bonner's stories contradicted truths proclaimed back in Washington, the government and its political allies attacked him and the *Times* as Communist sympathizers. Bonner was soon replaced by reporters far more willing to convey the official U.S. view of the war. (Years later, after Rosenthal retired, Bonner was hired back by the *Times*, where he works today.)

Press subservience in America has hardly been confined to the Reagan years, however, nor does it usually require overt government pressure. For example, long after Mr. Reagan left office in 1988, the media voluntarily kept offering astonishingly polite coverage of his dream of a missile defense system. I say polite because the coverage has rarely made clear the system's most embarrassing shortcoming: it cannot be built. For years, the system being developed failed even the so-called strapped-down chicken test: hitting a missile whose speed and trajectory were known in advance. Robert Park, a physicist at the University of Maryland and spokesman for the American Physical Society, points out that in the real world, missiles take evasive action and are masked by decoys, which makes hitting them "hopeless."

But belief in missile defense is an article of faith among the Republican right wing, not to mention stupendously lucrative for Raytheon and other corporations that benefit from contracts with the Pentagon—American taxpayers have poured $100 billion into missile defense so far, with another $238 billion projected through 2025—so the idea has enormous political momentum. In 1996 Democratic president Bill Clinton urged spending $13.5 billion more on missile defense before deciding, in 1999, whether to deploy it. American press coverage of his speech never pointed out that missile defense was a mirage; every story implicitly took it for granted that such a system could indeed be built. The press focused instead on Clinton's tactical differences with Senator Robert Dole, his Republican opponent in the upcoming fall election. Which man wanted to build a system faster? Who looked tougher on defense? How would swing voters respond?

The problem with the American press is not that it favors Republicans or Democrats; the problem is that it is a stenographer to power. In the name of objectivity and political neutrality, the Washington press corps limits its definition of quotable news sources to official Washington: administration officials, influential members of Congress, experts from the plethora of "think tanks" in town. This limits the range of debate to the existing Republican-to-Democrat spectrum. However valid a given point of view might be on an intellectual level—say, that missile defense is a technological pipe dream—if it isn't forcefully argued by a significant part of the Washington establishment, it receives no attention.

In short, the Washington press corps functions as a palace court press. It is adept at detailing the intrigues of palace politics: What is the president proposing? How will Congress react? Who is going to win the fight? Where does the balance of power lie? This is not unimportant information, but it falls short of what citizens really need to hold their government accountable. (It also makes reporters sound dumber than most of them actually are.) Because the press is not inclined to step outside the mind-set of the authorities it covers, it surrenders much of its formal independence and rarely acts as the check and balance on the nation's rulers that the founders envisioned.

A key corollary is that the press will be only as adversarial toward a given president as the opposition party is. Since journalists must (appear to) be neutral and quote mainly official sources, they depend on the opposition party to balance their coverage. If the opposition is tough, coverage of the president will be commensurately tougher. Other factors contribute to any president's media profile, but this rule of thumb accounts for much of the positive coverage that Reagan received; Democrats were simply unwilling to criticize him. Bill Clinton, on the other hand, endured fierce criticism virtually from the day he took office, largely because Republicans, especially on the extreme right, were out for blood.

And what of George W. Bush? Pre-inauguration, he seemed destined for a rough ride in the press; many Democrats were still furious over the Florida vote controversy. But no sooner had Bush taken office than Democratic congressional leaders let bygones be bygones and declared their faith in bipartisanship. Most Democrats joined in approving the centerpiece of Bush's agenda—a tax cut for corporations and the wealthy—so it was subjected to little media criticism. Coverage of the new president was, in short, relatively positive even before the September 11 tragedy catapulted his poll numbers to the stars and reduced Democrats and journalists alike to applauding members of the palace court chorus. Not until evidence emerged in May 2002 that his administration had mishandled clues that al-Qaida was planning a terrorist attack against the United States did Bush encounter tough media criticism, and then only because key sectors of the political elite—including, crucially, senior congressional Republicans—were suddenly demanding answers.

FLUFF-IN-MOUTH DISEASE

As recently as the late 1980s, what made a journalist radical (and rare) in the United States was a willingness to challenge the basic assumptions of the political and economic elites whose doings dominate most news coverage. Nowadays, it is a radical thing simply to be intelligent.

When I returned to the United States in 1995 after living abroad for five years, the single most striking change I noticed was that the media no longer took anything seriously. As I scanned the magazine rack at New York's Kennedy Airport, it seemed that virtually every cover featured a celebrity's face and every story line had a sex or lifestyle hook. Television was the worst—even *Nightline*, once the smartest news show around, was devoting nearly half of its shows to the O. J. Simpson trial—but newspapers had also succumbed to fluff-in-mouth disease. Since then, the trend has intensified. By 2001 the average thirty-minute evening newscast was devoting less than two minutes a night to international news. Bear in mind that television remains the primary source of most Americans' news and you begin to understand why we are bone ignorant about the rest of the world.

The American news media have degenerated over the past quarter century into a profit-obsessed colossus, a peddler of pseudo-news that at once entrances and demeans the public. The dumbing down of news stems from the monopolization of the media, and the consequently increased pressure for larger profits. "Most American corporations would be thrilled with a 10 percent profit margin, but most newspaper proprietors consider a 15 to 20 percent profit from their monopoly businesses a minimal sign of good health," wrote Leonard Downie Jr. and Robert G. Kaiser, two senior editors at the

Washington Post, in their 2002 book *The News About the News*. The preference for profits over professionalism is even stronger within television. Because pseudo-news pushes emotional buttons, it attracts bigger audiences. Because it needs little or no overseas news-gathering or in-depth knowledge, it costs less to produce. It also provokes fewer political repercussions, making it the product of choice among the business types who set the parameters for today's journalists.

The contrast with other advanced capitalist nations' media is instructive. Britain, France, Sweden, Germany, Italy, Japan—these nations, too, have tabloid newspapers and gimmicky TV news shows. But for the moment, an impressive array of more reliable news sources continues to dominate their media systems. In Germany, both of the leading weekly newsmagazines, *Der Spiegel* and *Focus*, are literally twice as thick each week as their American counterparts, because they are filled with more, and more intelligent, coverage of current affairs. The guiding assumption is that the route to profit and influence is to raise the magazine's quality, not lower it. Evening newscasts in Europe and Japan attract large audiences without descending to the "news you can use" fluff that dominates American broadcasts. They are able to be more serious in part because they are publicly owned and don't need to worry so much about ratings, or sacrifice one-third of their airtime to advertising. Norimichi Kobayashi, a Japanese exchange student who spent a year in the United States in 2001, told me that he was shocked by the commercialism and superficiality of American TV. "Even the PBS takes advertisement from Exxon," he wrote. "I was so dejected."

The American media used to be more serious and civic-minded, but that changed fast after the election of Ronald Reagan in 1980. In the name of free enterprise, Reagan deregulated the broadcasting business. Federal rules intended to ensure that the public interest was taken into account in the use of the nation's airwaves—which are, after all, public property—were relaxed or eliminated. Reagan's deregulation made renewal of broadcast licenses virtually automatic; no longer would companies have to earn their licenses by providing news and public affairs programming. Most lucrative of all, Reagan expanded ownership limits. Historically, federal law had limited a company to owning seven television stations, seven FM radio stations, and seven AM radio stations in the United States. In a democracy, the thinking went, no single voice should control too large a share of the communications system. Reagan said the market should decide; he wanted to eliminate restrictions entirely but had to settle for expanding the so-called 7-7-7 rule to 12-12-12. Those fifteen extra stations represented a gift to broadcast corporations of literally billions of dollars in additional revenues over the coming years.

Critics warned at the time that Reagan's deregulation might enrich media moguls but impoverish the nation, and so it has. The most obvious consequence is there onscreen: the mindless, manipulative drivel that now passes for news. The September 11 attacks sobered up American media for a few months, but by May 2002 the cable networks in particular were back to their old habits. When Robert Blake, an aging Hollywood actor, was accused of killing his young wife, CNN and its fellow travelers swarmed the story as if it were the next O. J. Simpson case, which they doubtless hoped it was.

Just as disturbing as this insulting definition of "breaking news" is what Americans don't see on television: any honest coverage of what the media corporations themselves are up to. General Electric, for example, not only owns the NBC television network but is a leading Pentagon contractor whose annual revenues dwarf the gross national product of entire countries. But GE's influence on people's lives all over the world will not be scrutinized on NBC; GE specifically forbade it after an NBC reporter was imprudent enough to try to report on GE's nuclear power operations. Likewise, when the top investigative reporter at ABC News prepared an unflattering report exposing employment of pedophiles at Disney World, the amusement park owned by ABC's parent, the Walt Disney Company, the report was rejected and never broadcast. *60 Minutes* sat on a damning story about the tobacco industry for fear that an industry lawsuit might jeopardize CBS's pending merger with Westinghouse Corporation, a scandal dramatized in the 1999 feature film *The Insider.*

Who polices the police? asks the old riddle of political philosophy. In 1996 the broadcast industry helped write a law that would fantastically enrich it and further expand its control over the American media system. Leaving even the 12-12-12 rule behind, the 1996 Telecommunications Act proposed increasing to one household in three the share of the national audience that any single broadcaster could reach. In addition, the act gave the industry $70 billion worth of new digital spectrum space—for free. This latter giveaway was too much even for the normally pro-business Bob Dole, who denounced it as corporate welfare in an opinion article for the *New York Times.* But ordinary Americans never heard a word about this betrayal of the public interest. The television networks broadcast not one report about the act, and Congress passed it overwhelmingly.

Deregulation continued to be all the rage under the Bush administration. The new chairman of the Federal Communications Commission, Michael Powell, signaled his disdain for safeguarding the public airwaves from corporate control by answering this way when asked how he defined the public interest: "The night after I was sworn in [as commissioner], I waited for a visit from the angel of the public interest. I waited all night, but she did not come." Powell wanted there to be absolutely zero restrictions on ownership of the airwaves—a single corporation could buy as many stations and cable outlets as it could pay for—and the federal courts appeared to agree. On February 19, 2002, an appeals court ordered the FCC to reconsider all such limits; it also struck down a regulation that restricted cable operators from owning television stations. Unless overturned by the Supreme Court, the ruling will open the door for Viacom, Walt Disney, AOL Time Warner, and other giants to gobble up what little remains of America's media diversity.

The American news media's ideological center of gravity has shifted well to the right over the past twenty years, in part because corporations have taken over virtually every news organization that reaches a mass audience, including such ostensibly noncommercial outfits as National Public Radio and the Public Broadcasting System. NPR and PBS have grown increasingly indistinguishable from commercial broadcasting since right-wing politicians successfully defunded them, beginning in the 1980s under Reagan and concluding during the Gingrich revolution of 1995, when members of Congress pressed to "zero out" their budgets. Left on starvation rations, NPR and PBS were forced to turn more and more to corporate funders, which in turn compelled them to produce programming likely to please those funders. Often this programming remains admirable on technical grounds, but it displays little critical distance from the centers of power in the United States, especially the giant corporations that dominate our economy and government. In April 2002 PBS broadcast "Commanding Heights," a documentary praising corporate globalization that was funded by such impartial sources as BP (formerly British Petroleum), FedEx, and Enron, though the latter was expunged from the show's credits after its corruption-stained bankruptcy in October 2001. "I wanna bite the hand that feeds me," sings Elvis Costello about media moguls who betray the public interest, "I wanna bite that hand so badly." But in the real world, few do.

"AN AMAZING LIE"

Americans now have the worst of both worlds: a press that, at best, parrots the pronouncements of the powerful and, at worst, encourages people to be stupid with pseudo-news that illuminates nothing but the bottom line. If you think I am painting too bleak a picture, how about this shocker: Not long before September 11, the press passed up—that is, missed—the story of Osama bin Laden's plan to attack the United States. That's right. America's corporate news organizations had the chance to blow the whistle on bin Laden's plans eight weeks in advance, but they chose not to run the story.

A year later, in 2002, the media swarmed all over the Bush administration for failing to heed warnings of an impending terrorist attack—pretty nervy, considering that the media had made exactly the same mistake. On June 23, 2001, a story reporting that "followers of exiled Saudi dissident Osama bin Laden are planning a major attack on U.S. and Israeli interests" was sent out over the Reuters wire service, which meant that it landed in virtually every major newsroom in the United States. United Press International circulated a similar report on June 25, informing subscribers that "Saudi dissident Osama bin Laden is planning a terrorist attack against the United States." But the stories were largely ignored by the nation's media. According to journalist Simon Marks, writing in *Quill*, the journal of the Society of Professional Journalists, "A search of the country's major newspaper and broadcast network Web sites reveals that barely any considered the stories worthy of publication."

Mind you, America's media found plenty of time during those same days to continue flogging a sex scandal involving Gary Condit, an obscure Democratic congressman, and to divulge the underage drinking arrest of President Bush's daughter Jenna. But a story about a Middle Eastern guy with a name Americans couldn't even pronounce, warning about an attack that might or might not happen? Who had time for that kind of trivia when there were vital issues of sex and drugs facing the nation? "I don't believe this is only a U.S. phenomenon," Marks later told me. "A decade ago, a man who is now one of the British television industry's leaders told me that he wanted me to make Russia sexy . . . an invitation I declined."

Would it have made any difference if the press had reported bin Laden's plans? Would such stories have sparked additional investigations or led to heightened alert on the part of federal authorities? We will never know. We only know the press couldn't be bothered to report the story in the first place—it was too busy chasing money.

As it was for many Americans, September 11 was a wake-up call for the nation's journalists. Although they never acknowledged their failure on the bin Laden story, the terror attacks did lead to much earnest talk about scaling back on fluffy news. And there was a brief, refreshing return to seriousness, even if the content did not always sparkle. After all, overseas bureaus had been closed and experienced reporters fired long ago; it was not easy to begin offering high-quality news about the outside world again. Besides, old habits die hard when underlying structures remain unchanged.

Especially on television and radio, the media's value system still preferred shock and bombast to clarity and reason. On October 7, a few hours before the United States launched its first aerial attacks on Afghanistan, the CNN White House correspondent literally shouted his report on the Bush administration's response to Taliban requests for more negotiations. Breathless and red-faced, the improbably named Major Garrett sounded no different than one of his Pentagon namesakes as he angrily declared that there would be no negotiations, time was up, the president had said no negotiations and that's what he meant.

Yelling was also routine on the analysis shows that were supposed to help viewers make sense of events. As their titles suggest, programs like *Crossfire*, *Hardball*, and *The Washington Gang* favor a macho approach; panelists bluster, insult and interrupt one another, and in general show all the wisdom and thought of a kennel of barking dogs. Their ideological cast is decidedly right-wing. Most panelists' views range from conservative to hard right; the left is defined by former Clinton administration officials.

Not all the post–September 11 coverage was idiotic; more intelligent fare was occasionally available from such elite print outlets as the *New York Times*, *Washington Post*, *Los Angeles Times*, and *Wall Street Journal*, as well as from National Public Radio and a few outposts of TV sanity such as PBS's *Frontline*. Timely and informative, the coverage revealed an impressive level of competence; there are skilled journalists working for these news organizations. The parts of the story they told—

what happened on September 11; how the nation was coping with its grief and fear; how the war in Afghanistan was being fought—were presented with authority and professionalism. The problem was, important parts of the story were missing. Some gaps resulted from the Bush administration's refusal to allow reporters to accompany American troops into war zones—part of a concerted effort to censor news that included pressuring news executives not to broadcast interviews with bin Laden and other adversaries. (Shouldn't Americans know as much as possible about their enemies?) The tragic story of *Wall Street Journal* reporter Daniel Pearl's abduction and murder in Pakistan illustrated the kinds of risks reporters willingly undertake to seek out the truth. It was all the more disingenuous, then, for the Pentagon to justify its battlefield restrictions on the grounds of concern for reporters' safety. When Doug Struck, a war correspondent for the *Washington Post*, tried to check out a tip that U.S. missiles had killed Afghan civilians in one village, U.S. soldiers prevented him— at gunpoint—from reaching the site. A Pentagon spokesman later claimed that Struck had been detained out of concern for his safety. The correspondent called this "an amazing lie," and he added, "It shows the extremes the military is going to . . . to keep reporters from finding out what's going on."

Such isolated instances aside, the press's traditional inclination to embrace Washington's perspective on foreign policy—an instinct heightened after September 11—reinforced the one-sided nature of most coverage. A study by Columbia University's Project for Excellence in Journalism, summarized by Bill Kovach and Tom Rosenstiel, found that "less than ten percent of the coverage evaluating administration policy offers significant dissent. Most contains no dissent at all." What media critic Michael Massing deplored in *The Nation* as "a

Soviet-style reliance on official and semi-official sources" further ensured that American policy and behavior were rarely cast in a less than glorious light.

Take the sensitive question of civilian casualties in Afghanistan. Yes, there were occasional mentions of the odd village here or there that suffered, but these were nestled in the crevices of larger stories that trumpeted the war's success. Not until most of the fighting was over and the Bush administration had won the public relations war did the *New York Times* publish, on February 10, a cumulative count of how many civilians had perished in Afghanistan. Overseas media, by contrast, paid close attention to the issue from the start, relying on their own reporters and also quoting a study by Marc Herold, a professor of economics at the University of New Hampshire, who collated news reports from Europe, India, and Pakistan to estimate the total civilian dead at over four thousand. Herold, who opposed the U.S. bombing campaign as "criminal," may have overstated his figures, but he was no more biased than the Pentagon officials whose earnest denials of civilian casualties were unskeptically quoted in American press accounts.

America's media should not reflexively oppose government policies, but they should widen their ideological perspective so that all meaningful points of view are covered. Almost never, for example, did the major media give space to advocates of nonmilitary responses to the September 11 attacks. While the op-ed pages of the *New York Times* and especially the *Washington Post* bristled day after day with calls for immediate bombing of Afghanistan and beyond, television producers explained the absence of alternative voices by saying that they couldn't find anyone who opposed war. They couldn't have looked very hard; by September 28 nearly two hundred prominent Americans, including the celebrities that television traditionally preferred (Martin Sheen and Bonnie Raitt), as well as internationally renowned intellectuals such as Edward W. Said and Frances Moore Lappé, had signed a statement calling for "Justice Not Vengeance." The statement was later published as an advertisement in various newspapers; in the United States, it seems, there are some things you have to buy the freedom to say.

The media did offer criticism of the war in Afghanistan, but only of its tactics, not its basic rationale. It was a good example of the palace court dynamic in action: because the Washington establishment was divided over how to conduct the war, the media ventilated these divisions at great length, through stories debating whether Bush's plan for air strikes would succeed, whether ground troops would be needed, whether the alliance would hold. Whether the war was justified, whether alternative responses might exist, whether September 11 should provoke a basic rethinking of America's approach to foreign affairs—these questions were simply not raised, much less discussed.

How different the world might be if the American people knew all the things their media keep from them! Less superficial and jingoistic coverage of foreign affairs would help Americans understand why their country's reputation overseas is so uneven. It would enable us to see foreigners not as incomprehensible, abstract stereotypes but as flesh-and-blood human beings with the same kinds of faults, virtues, and frailties that we have. Better reporting would explain why foreigners see the world differently, why they are so much more concerned about globalization than Americans are, why they are annoyed by Washington's environmental foot-dragging and imperial high-handedness, why they nevertheless generally yearn for friendlier relations with the United States. Improved journalism is no panacea; better information will not automatically yield better policies at home or increased cooperation abroad. But it is a vital first step. As long as America's media remain locked into their profiteering palace court posture, the American public is doomed to ignorance about the outside world, and that's not good for anyone.

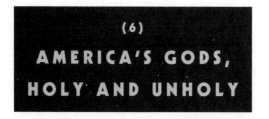

(6)

AMERICA'S GODS, HOLY AND UNHOLY

Paris, the Left Bank, a glorious morning in late May. The sunshine streaming onto the Boulevard Saint-Michel gives even the post office's blue-on-yellow logo a sparkling panache. Inside, lines of customers wait for service.

In walks a woman in her mid-forties with a harried look on her face and a college-age daughter in tow. She surveys the lines impatiently, then marches up to a window that is empty except for a sign reading "Fermé"—Closed. At a desk fifteen feet behind the window, a manager sits in deep concentration, counting out a stack of currency. The woman begins shouting in his direction in American English while waving a fistful of traveler's checks. "Hello, hello! Do you change these here?" The man looks up, startled; why is this woman shouting at him? His count ruined, he focuses on her continuing stream of questions and then replies, in halting English, "No, madame. I am sorry. This is the post office." The woman groans. "You don't change these? Why not? What do you change?" Other customers are rolling their eyes now, but the clerk remains courteous. Rising from his desk, he says, "The bank, madame, the bank, this way, on the Boulevard Saint-Michel." She is nearly wailing now: "Which is Saint-Michel? Out here?" Before he can assist further, she stomps out, without a thank-you, confiding to her daughter, "I gotta tell you, Jenny, I'm getting pretty frustrated here."

Maybe this woman was just having a bad day. Americans certainly have no monopoly on rude behavior abroad (the most obnoxious tourists I've encountered were a mob of English football fans who turned the red-light district of Amsterdam into an open-air latrine while singing racist ditties), and people of every country feel more comfortable when speaking their mother tongue. But no one has quite the sense of entitlement Americans do when it comes to speaking our own language. We import very few foreign-language books and movies, and non-English speakers rarely appear on our news broadcasts. Foreigners must adjust to us, we assume, not we to them.

This is our loss, I think. Many Europeans speak two if not three languages. In Africa, multilingualism is even more common. I remember a twelve-year-old in a dusty village in northern Kenya who spoke four languages: that of his mother's tribe, that of his father's, the Pan-African tongue of Swahili, and the English he learned in school. The boy saw nothing remarkable in this; he was prouder of the toy car that he had assembled from scrap wire and was steering around the village alleyways. Africans and Europeans aren't intrinsically smarter than Americans; they simply have incentives we lack. English reigns supreme in the United States, the rest of the world is far away, and when we do travel, the locals, increasingly, speak English (especially in Europe, where numerous transnational corporations, and even the German postal service, have made English their official working language). But if American travelers did learn a few local phrases—"Good morning," "Pardon me," "This food is delicious"—they would surely have a richer experience of the culture they were visiting.

Learning to stumble around in a new language takes time, however, and time is something Americans always feel short of. In the cobblestoned hill town of Montalcino, in Tuscany, there is a wine bar that has been open continuously since 1808. My waiter there was a quick-stepping, cheerful fellow who hailed from Morocco. We spoke in Italian, but I could hear from exchanges with other customers that his English was good. But, he confessed during a lull in the late afternoon rush, he sometimes had trouble with American customers. "Americans are always in a hurry," he complained. "They have fifteen minutes for wine tasting, fifteen minutes for the cathedral, and then they must leave for the next town. So they get impatient. They want their drinks right away, and they want the check before they even finish drinking. I wonder if they even taste the wine." (A grave error, for he was serving Brunello.)

Like so many things about one's homeland, the frenzied pace of American life is hard to recognize until one leaves it behind. I remember passing through San Francisco during my first trip around the world ten years ago. Needing a bottle of wine to bring to dinner with friends, I stopped in my old neighborhood shop and was immediately overwhelmed by the hundreds of choices available—I'd spent the preceding six months in eastern Africa and Thailand, where shops were simpler affairs. I finally made a selection and headed for the register to pay. But another customer saw me coming and sped up to get there first. He put his bottle on the counter without a word. The clerk, also silent, checked the price, punched it into the machine, and grunted the amount back to the customer, who already had his credit card out. The monosyllables they exchanged as they hurried through the transaction were in English, but I could barely follow along, I was so dumbstruck. I was still attuned to African rhythms; in Africa, a clerk and customer acting this way would be considered not so much rude as crazy. No eye contact, no hello, no chatting about one another's health or anything else—in African eyes, this would qualify as barbaric behavior.

Again, it's not that Africans are inherently nicer people; Americans are plenty friendly under the right circumstances. The difference is that Africans live in social conditions that encourage interchange, discourage hurry, and elevate the common good over that of the individual. In a pre-industrial society, time is measured by the arc of the sun and the turning of the seasons. There is time to talk because no one is going anywhere (and anyway, rushing is foolish in the hot and humid climates that characterize much of Africa). African life should not be romanticized; there are fewer of the appointments, diversions, and obligations that define most American lives, but there are also fewer opportunities to escape the limits of tradition: everyone has known each other all their lives, and there are all the jealousies, deceptions, and other human weaknesses common to any society. But anchoring everything is an unshakable sense of community. People have survived hard times in the past because they have actively cooperated, sharing food and other scarce items in the knowledge that their peers will share with them if and when bad times come. Chitchat, communal solidarity, and a leisurely pace are matters of self-interest in Africa. In America, it's every man for himself, and don't slow down or you'll be left behind.

"When I visited America, it was very different from here,"

Gina, a young office worker in Cairo, told me. "Americans are not aggressive like Germans; they're nice, open people. But they are very individualistic. Divorce rates are fifty percent, and I think it is because people put their individual desires first. Parents don't know much about their children, and if they tell the kids not to do something, it doesn't matter; they do it anyway. Here, family is more important and we spend more time with friends. My impression is Americans are lonelier, more stressed and depressed, because they don't have the social networks we do."

"I think most French people admire America for its dynamism and creativity, but they also have reservations about Americans," said Laurent Joffrin, the editor of *Le Nouvel Observateur*. "They think Americans are too tough, for example—that they place too high a value on money and not enough on less material aspects of life, such as family and community. If given the chance, most French would not choose the American lifestyle. They may copy some American habits, like going to McDonald's or buying bigger cars, but for the most part they prefer the French way of doing things."

Family mealtimes, for example, are primary bonding rituals in France (and most of the world), but scheduling conflicts and eat-on-the-run convenience are displacing them in the United States. "My thirteen-year-old granddaughter spent a few weeks with family friends in America this summer, and she was surprised to discover that the four girls and their parents rarely shared a family meal together," said Susan George, a leading French intellectual. "Everyone ate on their own, raiding the refrigerator and heating up prepackaged food in the microwave." Bruno Rebelle, the director of Greenpeace France, says that the French are much more critical of genetically modified food than Americans are simply because the two cultures view food differently. "In the United States," he quips, "food is fuel. Here, it's a love story."

Americans take a similarly utilitarian attitude toward architecture and public space. I'm often discouraged upon returning home from a foreign trip to confront the ugliness and uniformity of America's automobile-centric landscape. The United States is still beautiful in many places, especially its open spaces, but as suburbs have proliferated and consumerism increased, much of our public space has been blighted by seemingly endless strips of mega-malls, fast-food outlets, discount chains, gas stations, and parking lots. Indistinguishable from one another, these monuments to homeliness have drained communities of their former charm and individuality, offering the appearance of choice and convenience even as they homogenize our culture and deaden our spirit.

Television, which dominates our lives inside the home, has much the same effect. Television is America's favorite drug, and we consume more of it than anyone else on earth. Most households boast two or more television sets, at least one of which is switched on an average of seven hours a day, even though there's so little worth watching. As Bruce Springsteen sang a few years ago, "Fifty-seven channels and nothing on." But television is part of the family; we love it and hate it at the same time. Time-stressed parents use it as a free babysitter. Older folks and shut-ins rely on it as a companion and link to the outside world. Viewers of all ages talk fondly about "zoning out" or "channel surfing" in front of the set after a hard day; it's a soothing antidote to all our running around.

We know that too much television isn't good for you; we even joke about TV being the "boob tube." Studies show that the human brain is more active when asleep than when absorbing television broadcasts; thus we exercise far less critical judgment toward what we watch than what we read. Such passivity is dangerous when so much of American politics takes place on screen. Equally unsettling is our growing allegiance to the values conveyed by television: violence, consumerism, greed, exhibitionism, conflict. The average twelve-year-old has seen eight thousand murders on television, and studies suggest that such viewing leads to increased aggression and violent crime later in life. There are moments when American television rises above the muck to offer amusing, enlightening programming, but these are rare; the medium's central purpose is to capture eyeballs and sell products, so hype and humbug generally triumph over wit and wisdom. Our addiction to television has debased our culture, dulled our minds, and encouraged our society's splintering into isolated individualism, but we seem powerless to break the habit.

BUILDING BETTER MOUSETRAPS

After Sigmund Freud returned from visiting the United States, in 1908, he complained so incessantly about its lack of taste and culture that an acquaintance asked why he hated the place so. "Hate America?" replied Freud. "I don't hate America, I regret it! I regret that Columbus ever discovered it!" The father of psychoanalysis was one of many foreigners who have thought Americans may be rich but they sure don't know how to enjoy it. Americans are friendly but boorish, clever but shallow, prosperous but lonely. They are drowning in material possessions but poor in family, friends, and community. They are oddly moralistic; they seem to find sex shameful but violence beautiful. Above all, they live to work rather than work to live. The American norm of two weeks' vacation a year strikes Europeans as uncivilized masochism. "We insist on our vacations!" I was told by Detlef Schulz, a Swedish social worker who looked like the twin of the English actor Alec Guinness. "Life is too short to spend it working all the time."

True enough. But the forces that make Americans the world's worst workaholics (except, perhaps, for the Japanese) are deeply rooted—in our history, in the values we have been taught since childhood, in the economic structures and technological forces that are propelling our civilization relentlessly forward—toward what, we cannot say. Americans, I should point out, don't necessarily like all this; it's simply what we've gotten used to. Some of us find it exhausting to live in a society where time seems always to be speeding up, where every new gadget—e-mail, cell phones, Palm Pilots—promises us more freedom and convenience but also further separates us from the larger community and our inner selves. We complain about stress (and gobble $800 million worth of drugs a year to compensate), we resent not having enough time with our kids, we can be nostalgic for our rural past and its calmer ways. But in the end, we are creatures of our society, and we neither recognize the full damage being done to us nor see any real alternative.

The heart of the problem is revealed in the signature American saying, "Time is money." From the beginning, the chief ambition of our civilization has been the unbridled pursuit of wealth, so the time available for other aspects of life has been correspondingly reduced. Meanwhile, our dominant religion, Protestantism, has preached a work ethic that instills guilt in anyone not striving to get ahead. The results have been, in some respects, admirable. The supreme value assigned to money and its pursuit has made the American economy remarkably dynamic and brought forth inventions and innovations that have transformed the world. But we have also been impoverished in definite, albeit less quantifiable, ways.

Well before the United States was founded, the American continent was seen as a place to seek one's fortune. The dream of striking it rich led the Spanish explorer Coronado to become the first visitor to the "new" world in 1540; he spent the next three years searching for the apocryphal Seven Cities of Gold. Pilgrims came in 1620 seeking religious freedom, but most other European immigrants came in hopes of making money. The pursuit of wealth was a driving motivation behind the entire settlement of the United States, with farmers and trappers spreading ever westward throughout the nineteenth century. The frontier was a dangerous place, but land was essentially free if you could survive, and that was a powerful lure. Dreams of treasure also sparked the single biggest, fastest migration in our history, the Gold Rush of 1849 that drew millions to California, just as it was hopes for a better life that propelled the great waves of European immigration to America around the turn of the twentieth century.

The fondness for guns that today distinguishes America from other nations likewise has its roots in our economic history, for use of force was integral to our pursuit of wealth. Foreigners find it barbaric and frightening that average citizens are allowed to carry guns in America, even with permits, and they see the nation's high rates of crime, school shootings, and murders as a predictable result of this freedom. (And gun purchases increased sharply after September 11.) Our enthusiasm for the death penalty also baffles many, especially in Europe. But a culture of guns and violence took hold early in the United States, and it has never been eclipsed. On the frontier, a man could keep only what he could defend, and since he was often displacing Native Americans, defense was a frequent necessity. Other settlers also were a threat. Just as liberty existed in the United States before authority did, so firearms were ubiquitous before effective law enforcement emerged. Quarrels over property lines or water rights could well end with shots exchanged, and robbery was common in the Wild West, especially around mining towns where fortunes were being amassed in broad daylight.

When Oscar Wilde visited the United States in the 1890s, he gave a lecture in Leadville, Colorado, supposedly the richest town in the world at the time. He was preceded onstage by a first act: two local men accused of murder were tried and executed on the spot before a large crowd. Shaken, Wilde went ahead with his lecture on the ethics of art, drawing on *The Autobiography of Benvenuto Cellini.* He later wrote to friends that his audience "seemed much delighted, but I was reproved . . . for not having brought [Cellini] with me. I explained that he had been dead for some little time, which elicited the inquiry: 'Who shot him?' "

Irony and subtlety were little valued on the frontier; Americans were hearty, open people who were unashamed of their lust for wealth. Countless visitors have remarked on Americans' tendency to value things according to their monetary worth. "Americans are satisfied with things because they are large; and if not large, they must have cost a great deal of money," British diplomat Lepel Henry Griffin observed in the 1880s. "The two houses most beautiful architecturally in the Michigan Avenue at Chicago were shown to me as half-a-million-dollar houses. A horse is not praised for his points, but as having cost so many thousand dollars."

If Americans were unduly proud of their money, perhaps it was because they often had made it themselves. In Europe, wealth tended to be inherited, and social mobility was extremely restricted: the class you were born into was generally the class you died in, and your children, too. Options were sometimes limited even within families of means; law and tradition in some cases dictated that the oldest son inherit all of a father's property, leaving the others with nothing. And when inheritances were evenly divided, the individual shares could be too small to sustain a livelihood. In these cases, America beckoned as a risky but exciting opportunity. Its frontier was open, its riches available to anyone with the grit to grab them through courage and hard work. In the United States, pursuit of wealth was democratized, thrown open to all comers, and let the best man win.

Business therefore became more respected in America than it had been in Europe. The landed aristocracy who dominated European ruling circles disparaged business as an undignified pursuit; after all, it meant a life of work rather than leisure. In the United States, business carried no bad odor; it was the door to economic advancement. Ingenuity and enterprise could be as important as start-up capital: find a way to make a product better or cheaper than the competition and you could capture his customers. Or you could create an altogether new product that people desired so much they would pay handsomely for it.

Thus salesmanship became a central element of American business; if a product couldn't actually be *made* better, at least it could be made to *sound* better. It's no coincidence that the United States eventually became the world's leader in advertising, public relations, and marketing—or that smooth-talking dreamers and charming con artists figure so prominently in our national ethos, from the doomed Willy Loman in Arthur Miller's *Death of a Salesman*, to the hilarious tricksters of Mark Twain (starting with Tom Sawyer, who dupes neighborhood children into whitewashing a fence by pretending the job is beyond them), to circus impresario P. T. Barnum, who famously boasted, "There's a sucker born every minute."

Americans' passion to get rich also put a premium on practicality; if an idea didn't make money, what good was it? The value of any knowledge lay in its application, a conviction elaborated in more exalted terms by William James in *Pragmatism*, the 1907 book that ranks as perhaps the most important contribution to philosophy made by an American. Leave lofty theory to others; Americans want to build a better mousetrap.

The modern world is awed by America's scientific accomplishments, but it is applied science—technology—that is our true genius, as evidenced by the many epoch-making inventions that originated in the United States. Our first important innovation came in 1807, when Robert Fulton created the first commercially practical steamboat, which opened the nation's waterways to large-scale trade, driving the industrialization and westward expansion that signaled America's growth into an economic giant. Cyrus McCormick's invention of the reaper in 1834 revolutionized agriculture, increasing the efficiency of wheat harvesting twentyfold. Two years later, John Deere's invention of the steel plow made hard soil cultivable, laying a foundation for the Midwest to become the breadbasket of the world. In 1844 Samuel F. B. Morse invented the telegraph, connecting the far-flung nation's east and west coasts. Later, Americans developed arguably the two most important technological advances of the entire century: Alexander Graham Bell's patent of the telephone in 1876, and Thomas Edison's invention of the electric lamp in 1879.

In the new century, Wilbur and Orville Wright became the first to succeed at flying an airplane, in 1903. In 1911 Frederick Taylor revolutionized manufacturing by breaking factory tasks into discrete steps and assigning each step to a specific worker; Taylorism gave rise to the assembly line perfected by Henry Ford, yielding fantastic productivity increases but reducing workers to bored, interchangeable cogs in the machine. As the century continued, American business funded more and more scientific research and was rewarded with breakthroughs that created whole new industries: radio, television, movies, plastics, antibiotics and a staggering array of other medical developments, as well as nuclear energy, electronics, X rays, and computers. Besides generating huge direct profits for their parent firms, these breakthroughs boosted productivity throughout the American economy, raised living standards, spurred exports, and transformed modern civilization.

The crowning achievement came in 1969, when the United States won the race against the Soviet Union to land a man on the moon. "Seeing America go to the moon made a powerful impression on Egyptians, at least of my generation," the journalist and scholar Abdel Monem Said Aly told me in Cairo. "It was a very impressive demonstration of America's scientific and economic might." The moon race also spurred development of the satellite, computer, and cyber-technologies that are shaping the world of the twenty-first century—and further accelerating the hectic pace of daily life.

"Every day in our newspapers there are stories about American inventions and Nobel Prize winners," Aly noted. "There is suspicion among some Egyptians that America wants to exploit us through its technology," he added, "but I don't agree. I have Bill Gates's word processing program in my computer, and I benefit a lot from it. I honestly don't see where he is exploiting me."

Bill Gates may be the ultimate symbol of American as philistine: a computer geek whose obsessive focus on software has left him famously lacking in social skills but—no small matter—also made him the richest man in the world. And the cyber-revolution that exploded out of Seattle and Silicon Valley in the 1990s is but one aspect of America's continuing technological preeminence. American researchers are at the forefront of the genetic engineering revolution that for better or worse may soon transform everything from agriculture to human and animal reproduction. Americans are also prominent in the biomedical research that could extend human life spans by enabling us to replace worn-out limbs and organs as easily as we now replace the engines and brake systems of our cars. We Americans are a clever bunch. Not always wise, for wisdom implies weighing the consequences of a given technology and perhaps deciding not to pursue it. But certainly clever.

"IN GOD WE TRUST"

All this suggests a great irony: How did America become the wealthiest, most technologically advanced society in history while remaining probably the most religious country in the industrialized world? After all, the New Testament is full of warnings against accumulating wealth ("It is easier for a camel to go through the eye of a needle than for a rich man to enter into the kingdom of God"). And in most industrialized countries, the rise of science during the past two centuries inexorably reduced the influence of the church as breakthroughs in cosmology, geology, chemistry, and physics undermined such literal readings of the Bible as the belief that the earth was created in seven days some four thousand years ago. But in the United States, money, science, and faith flourish side by side.

Religion's role in American life is often underestimated within mainstream American discourse, perhaps because much of the nation's intelligentsia, including the media, favor a secular world view. But leave New York City and other islands of cosmopolitanism behind and the pervasive influence of religion in the American heartland is unmistakable. Religion's hold is especially strong in the South and Midwest, and among Hispanic and African-American communities. The ubiquity of bumper stickers ranging from the cheerful ("Honk If You Love Jesus") to the foreboding ("The Lord Is Coming, Are You Ready?") suggests the underlying attitudes. A remarkable 94 percent of Americans believe in God. The vast majority of us—85 percent—are Christians, and half of those call themselves born-again Christians, because they feel they were figuratively reborn after accepting Jesus Christ as their personal savior. Jesus is an active presence in such individuals' lives, and it is absolutely common for them, when confronting a large or small life decision, to ask, "What would Jesus do?" Many, though by no means all, born-again Christians are fundamentalists who believe followers of other religions are doomed to eternal damnation. The United States is the largest market for religious books in the world, and one of the biggest sellers over the past five years has been the "Left Behind" series: eight novels that dramatize the Rapture theory of salvation. Favored by many fundamentalists, this theory holds that when conditions cited in the Book of Revelations come to pass, God will end the world in an explosion of light—the Rapture—and sweep twelve thousand Christians up to heaven while condemning the rest of humanity to hell.

It's not surprising that religion matters so much in the United States; it was one of the main reasons the country was settled in the first place. And from the earliest days, there was tension over its proper role in society. In one camp were the Puritans, stern Protestants who came to America for religious freedom, then promptly tried to outlaw all other religions. In the other camp were the Pilgrims, also Protestants but less dogmatic; they allowed the unconverted to take part in communal decision-making. The decisive blow was struck by the founders, whose belief in tolerance was so steadfast that they omitted the word "God" from our Constitution. Determined to avoid the religious-based wars and power struggles that had bloodied Europe and other lands for centuries, the founders mandated strict separation of church and state and complete freedom of religion. In theory, this included the freedom to hold no religion, though this perspective was alien to the founders themselves, all of whom (except Madison) were firm theists.

Separation of church and state in America has never been as absolute as our rhetoric implies, however, and the battle between fundamentalism and tolerance still rages. Churches of all faiths are exempted from paying property taxes—a subsidy to religion worth countless billions of dollars per year. Every piece of money in the United States bears the motto "In God We Trust." And our legal, political, and educational systems are regularly roiled by disputes over evolution, abortion, prayer in school, and kindred issues. Like their Puritan forebears, many modern-day fundamentalists believe that their version of Christian teachings should be reflected in the nation's laws and practices. Their zeal is unshaken by smirking news media coverage of efforts to ban Harry Potter novels for their supposedly satanist content (twenty-six such challenges were mounted in sixteen states in 1999) or delete evolution from the public school curriculum in favor of creationism. As it happens, most Christians accept evolution, tolerate homosexuality, and hold diverse views on abortion, but the power of a determined extremist minority can be significant. Prayer in school, repeatedly rejected by the courts as a violation of church-state separation, is now being pushed under its new name—"a moment of silence." In March 2001 a member of the Ohio Board of Education forced hearings on whether to teach "intelligent design," the updated version of creationism, in the state's classrooms. The final vote went against her, but similar initiatives are likely elsewhere; for proponents, it's a matter of faith.

And that faith is shared by high-powered politicians in Washington. George W. Bush, who cited Jesus Christ when asked to name his favorite philosopher, is a "born-again" believer who happens to owe fundamentalists a major political debt. Hoping to gain decisive influence in the White House, leaders of the Christian right decided early in the 2000 presidential race to throw their weight behind Bush rather than the unabashed evangelical Gary Bauer. Bush has repaid the favor by pressing his "faith-based" initiative to transfer social welfare responsibilities from government to churches, and by appointing judges and federal officials sympathetic to fundamentalists' concerns. Although the Christian right's power has declined since its glory days in the 1990s, when it was key to the right-wing takeover of Congress and the impeachment of President Clinton, it remains a significant grassroots force, especially in the South, where few Republicans are elected without its help. Among its allies are the two most powerful Republicans on Capitol Hill, Senate Minority Leader Trent Lott and House whip Tom DeLay, who spearheaded Clinton's impeachment by drawing on the outrage of millions of Christians who regarded the president's extramarital affair as a stain on the nation's virtue. Democrats declare their religious bona fides no less than Republicans, however; it is inconceivable that a candidate from either party could win election in the United States if he or she admitted to being an atheist. Both Clinton and Al Gore were proud to call themselves "born-again" Baptists, and Clinton relied on Christian rituals of confession and forgiveness when trying to resuscitate his reputation after the Lewinsky scandal.

Religion is key to understanding much about the United States, including our reputation as philistines (a word drawn from the Bible, as it happens). Americans chase wealth with a single-minded obsessiveness that strikes foreigners as coarse, yet we see ourselves as morally upright, God-fearing people. As is often the case when pondering America's paradoxes, the key to the mystery was supplied long ago by Tocqueville, who wrote, "Never have I been so conscious of the influence of religion on the morals and social and political state of a people as since my arrival in America." A strong religious faith, the young Frenchman argued, was no contradiction to the "passion to get rich" that was Americans' chief priority in life. On the contrary, religion was an essential counterweight, for it purified the lust for money and made it morally respectable. "They will never succeed in preventing men from loving wealth," Tocqueville wrote, "but they may be able to induce them to use only honest means to enrich themselves."

Tocqueville did miss one crucial part of the equation: the Calvinist tint of American Protestantism. Calvinism put an extra twist on Americans' pursuit of wealth, for it prescribed hard work for everyone and held that an unquestioning faith in God—rather than good works—was the only path to salvation. The possession of riches was a sign that God favored a given individual, just as a person's poverty signaled God's disapproval (and the person's unenviable prospects in the afterlife).

Calvinism has been central to American morality for so long that these attitudes have been absorbed even by Americans who are not fervently religious. Affluent individuals believe they are well-off because they deserve it, not because, as is usually the case, they were born into such advantages as prosperous parents, good health, the guarantee of a college education, and the like. There is a joke that used to be told about President Bush the first, and is now told about his son: "He was born on third base and thinks he hit a triple."

The idea that we are rich because we are morally good is convenient in many ways, and it may have been psychologically essential in the country's early years, when whites needed to assure themselves that stealing Native Americans' land and enslaving Africans were not mortal sins. But today, this deep-seated cultural assumption manifests itself in Americans' believing we cannot be good unless we are working hard and getting ahead. One reason that many of us are workaholics is that putting in long hours convinces us, and others, that we are good people. This assumption also helps explain our attitudes toward the poor, which often tend more toward fear and contempt than compassion and generosity.

Being poor, in many Americans' eyes, is the poor's own fault. Of course, religious faith in the United States has always been about more than rationalizing one's economic ambitions. Individual believers have looked to the church for spiritual solace and fellowship. Various denominations have played honorable, sometimes courageous roles in helping the poor and combating social injustice; black churches, for example, were the heart of the civil rights movement, and progressive Catholics have agitated against poverty. Meanwhile, the religious tolerance insisted upon by the founders continues to bear fruit today in the form of perhaps the most diverse religious landscape in the world; some thirty-seven thousand different forms of faith are practiced in the United States. Despite harsh words and legal conflicts over the years, we have never suffered the kind of religious bloodshed that many other countries have. In today's world, that is no small accomplishment.

Our challenge for the future is, again, to remember our history. As religious-based conflict threatens to engulf the world, the United States' example of relative religious peace illustrates the benefits of (even imperfect) separation of church and state, and the religious freedom and tolerance that flow from it. America has many gods, holy and unholy. For every one of us who prays to Jesus, Allah, Yahweh, or Buddha, there is another who bows before the altars of television, techno-wizardry, and the almighty dollar; indeed, many of us see no contradiction in choosing gods from each of these lists. Americans embrace a dizzying, untidy mix of sacred and secular faiths that often pull us in conflicting directions, leaving us at once vulgar yet devout, modern yet old-fashioned, self-righteous yet rootless. This spiritual melting pot, for all its contradictions, seems far superior to the beguiling certainties advanced by fundamentalists of any stripe. "A foolish consistency is the hobgoblin of little minds," said Emerson, and the point still holds. The world is getting smaller by the day, and the era now unfolding demands as supple a vision of reality as we can imagine.

7

THE LAND OF OPPORTUNITY
TURNS SELFISH

There is no more American a story, at least for today's generations, than *The Wizard of Oz*; it's the closest thing we have to a national fairy tale. Virtually all of us have seen *The Wizard of Oz* on television from the time we were four or five years old. Mention the Yellow Brick Road, the Wicked Witch of the West, or Emerald City, or hum a few notes of "Over the Rainbow" or "We're Off to See the Wizard," and Americans of all ages, races, and classes will catch the reference immediately, and with fondness.

Today's kids watch *The Wizard of Oz* on video, which means they watch it whenever they want, and often over and over. When I was growing up in the 1960s, watching *The Wizard of Oz* was more of a special event, even a national ritual. Once a year, usually around Easter, it was shown on network television. My brothers and sisters and I, and most of our friends, looked forward to that night for days. Like countless other families across the nation, we would gather in front of the television with popcorn and hot chocolate and be spellbound yet again by the adventures of Dorothy, the Kansas farm girl whose house is lifted off the ground by a terrifying tornado, spun through the skies, and dropped—on top of a witch!—in the land of Oz. Our parents, who kept us company on these evenings (especially during the scary parts), could recall having first seen *The Wizard of Oz* in actual movie theaters. Released in 1939, Hollywood's adaptation of L. Frank Baum's novel made Judy Garland an instant star and earned the movie a permanent place in the American consciousness.

The movie entices all ages because it works on all levels, and its appeal has endured because it both reflects and articulates some of our basic national beliefs. The movie is dedicated to "the Young in Heart," and Americans are certainly that: sometimes naïve, but charmingly optimistic and well-meaning, and suckers for a happy ending. Very young viewers are entranced by the movie's vivid images—the silver Tin Man rusted beneath talking apple trees, the flying monkeys descending from the sky to kidnap Dorothy and her dog Toto—and by its easy-to-follow songs, especially as sung by the squeaky-voiced Munchkins. Older kids are drawn by the story's classic structure: the quest, in which a young person journeys forth into the world and faces tests that help her grow into adulthood. And the story works on grown-ups because it combines humor, song, and fantasy with uplifting moral purpose. Like Oz, our world contains evil as well as beauty, and the Wizard's command—to bring him the broomstick of the Wicked Witch of the West—sounds no less imposing than some challenges demanded of us.

What very few Americans realize is that the movie is also a political parable. Direct testimony on this point came years after the fact from E. Y. "Yip" Harburg, who wrote the movie's song lyrics. He and his songwriting partner, composer Harold Arlen, were active leftists who supported President Franklin

Roosevelt's New Deal programs for poor and working-class Americans devastated by the Depression. "Of course Emerald City was the New Deal!" said Harburg, referring to the gleaming green palace that is Dorothy's goal throughout the film. (When she finally arrives, a welcoming song describes a veritable worker's paradise where "we get up at noon and start to work by one, take an hour for lunch and then at two we're done.")

Neither the songwriters nor the script is ever heavy-handed, but the signs are there for those who care to read them. Dorothy and her companions form a sort of composite of the average American: Dorothy represents the nation's innocent yet optimistic spirit; the Scarecrow represents farmers, who still made up nearly half of the population in 1939; the Tin Man stands for workers—the industrial man who emerged with the nation's shift to manufacturing in the early twentieth century. The Cowardly Lion is harder to interpret; perhaps he represents soldiers in service to their country, perhaps he is simply a comic figure. But there is no mistaking the movie's villain. In her Kansas incarnation, she is a heartless capitalist who threatens Dorothy's family with a lawsuit "that will take your whole farm" if Toto isn't put to death. As the Wicked Witch of the West, she personifies greed, hissing at Dorothy like an impatient landlord, "I can't wait forever to get my hands on those [ruby] slippers."

Even if one disregards the symbolism, the message of *The Wizard of Oz* is clear: Believe in yourself, stick by your friends, fight for what's right, and things will get better. Dorothy and her companions spend most of the movie pinning their hopes on the Wizard: she thinks she needs his help to get back home to Kansas, the Scarecrow wants a brain, the Tin Man a heart, the Lion some courage. In the end, the four learn that only they can provide such things—indeed, they already possess them, they just didn't believe in themselves enough to see it. Perhaps originally meant to encourage Depression-era Americans to demand the better life that was rightfully theirs, *The Wizard of Oz* continues to resonate today because it touches something deep and enduring in the American soul: our faith that we live in a land where, as Dorothy sings, "the dreams that you dare to dream really do come true."

TASTING THE GOLDEN APPLE

Foreigners share this view of America as an almost magical place where anything is possible. I think immediately of a comment I heard from a barman in Sicily: "Everyone thinks about America." The man delivered his pronouncement with a magnificent shrug, as if to underline the inevitability of America's appeal. He was solidly built, with graying hair combed back on a squarish head. He lived in Agrigento, a city on Sicily's southern coast that boasts some of the finest Greek ruins in all the Mediterranean, so there was a steady tourist business. But to make ends meet, the barman had to work six days a week, and he was stuck in this job, probably for the rest of his life. "It's not like that in America, is it?" he asked. "In America, one day you are working here, the next day you decide to work somewhere else. If you don't like that job, you find another one. Things aren't like that here, jobs are hard to find." To cross the ocean and start anew in the United States was tempting, he added, but unrealistic. He spoke no English and was no longer young. Besides, who would take care of his bar? But he had thought about it, yes, he had thought about it. Everyone thinks about America.

This gentleman may have romanticized conditions in the United States, but he knew the realities of his own country well enough. A couple of days later, as I stepped inside the Monreale cathedral outside Palermo, I couldn't believe my eyes. What was Roberto Benigni doing here, greeting visitors? A closer look revealed a man who simply bore an uncanny resemblance to the great Italian comic. Soft-spoken but wearing a loud red sport jacket, he was offering tours of the cathedral, conducted in Italian or Sicilian dialect. Brilliant mosaics in dozens of colors covered every inch of the interior, and as the man elucidated the scenes they depicted (designed to teach the Bible to illiterate peasants), it was clear he knew his subject backward and forward. He had been coming to the cathedral all his life, he explained, but offering tours only over the past two years. Before that, he was a stonemason—hence his love of mosaics—until a sprained back left him unemployable. "Disability payments are very low in Sicily, so I had to devise an alternative," he said. A humble alternative it was. Prohibited from competing with official guides, he could not charge a set fee, only accept donations. When he learned I came from San Francisco, he surprised me with his knowledge of both the city's past and its present. "Ah, San Francisco," he said with a gentle smile. "The city of gold and Internet."

These two men were far from the poorest individuals I've met in my travels. But precisely because they belonged to the relatively prosperous working class of Europe, their perspectives shed light on an apparent contradiction to criticisms of the United States: If America is as flawed as detractors say—if it is a self-centered, gluttonous bully with a racist past and a soulless center—why are millions of people from around the world willing to do nearly anything to immigrate here? Why do campesinos risk death from heat and thirst to cross the deserts of northern Mexico into the United States? Why do Asian workers invest their life savings in bribes and cram into fetid cargo compartments for perilous ocean voyages to America? Why do document-clutching hopefuls stand in the bitter cold for hours outside the United States embassy in Moscow just to get an appointment to make a visa request that will likely be denied? The answer is obvious: Conditions in the United States look vastly preferable to the circumstances these people face at home. Just because foreigners criticize America doesn't mean they don't want to taste the golden apple themselves.

The United States has, of course, always been a nation of immigrants. And although our reputation as the home of freedom is justified, in fact most immigrants have come here to better themselves economically. America was, and still is, seen as the land of opportunity, where anyone willing to work hard can get ahead, because rewards depend on merit, not connections. It might take a generation or two, but your family too can join the American middle class and live happily ever after.

Millions and millions of immigrants have lived exactly this scenario: sacrifice, save, invest in the children's education, and watch them achieve a better life. (Of course, many others have worked just as hard but never gotten ahead; there are no guarantees in America.) Ricardo Morales, for example, works a construction job in Chicago. The $100 a week that he sends to his family is part of $9.3 billion in wage remittances that Mexican immigrants in the United States send home every year to buy food and other necessities for their families and to build roads and water systems for their communities. Among the material deprivations Morales accepts in return is sharing a one-bedroom apartment with four other men. "Our thinking," he told the *New York Times*, "is that we will make sacrifices now so that our families can live better and so that one day we can live better back home."

Viewed from afar, the American economy looks healthy; by world standards, our growth rate is high and unemployment low. Jobs are relatively easy to find, just as the Agrigento barman imagines. What neither foreigners nor affluent Americans always appreciate is how poorly paid many of these jobs are, relative to what things cost in the United States. Morales is one of the lucky ones; as a roofer, he earns approximately $12.50 an hour—more than double the federally mandated minimum wage of $5.15 an hour—and when he sends his dollars to Mexico, they buy much more than they would in the United States. But, as Barbara Ehrenreich reports in *Nickel and Dimed*, her magnificent account of working undercover in the late 1990s at unskilled jobs such as housecleaner and waitress, 30 percent of the American workforce earned $8 or less an hour in 1998. For them, dingy, crowded apartments, crappy processed food, and unaffordable health care are inescapable realities.

The 1990s were portrayed by the American news media as a gloriously prosperous era when the rise of the Internet and other information technologies was upending traditional economic assumptions and fueling a stock market boom that could make all Americans, even blue-collar factory workers, rich. This was a cruel deception. The stock market did boom in the 1990s, and many millionaires were created, but the overwhelming share of the profits went to the upper crust of our population. True, half of all Americans were invested in the stock market, generally through retirement plans over which they had little control, but they were small-time players. The vast majority of stocks—89 percent—were owned by the richest 10 percent of American households, and they benefited proportionally. By 1999 Bill Gates alone owned as much wealth as the bottom 40 percent of Americans. The soaring stock markets did not democratize wealth, they concentrated it.

Data on income tell the same story: the 1990s were a spectacularly rewarding decade for the highest-earning 20 percent of Americans (and especially the top 5 percent), because they captured the lion's share of income generated by the stock market boom. Incomes rose for other income groups as well, but by much less. The bottom 80 percent—America's poor, working- and middle-class majority—did not even manage to recover the economic ground they had lost during the past two decades. By the end of the 1990s, American workers were still earning less in real terms than when Richard Nixon left the White House in 1973, even though their productivity had increased by one-third in the meantime.

The American Dream offers the promise that if you work hard, you—or at least your children—will be rewarded with a better life. Today, more and more Americans are working longer hours than ever, but they are not necessarily getting ahead. The American middle class is shrinking, both in absolute size and in purchasing power, while the top and bottom classes are expanding. Increasingly, the United States is dividing between a small, fabulously wealthy elite and a growing, struggling majority who must work hard simply not to fall behind.

Nevertheless, America's reputation as a land of opportunity remains intact overseas, and not just among uninformed laymen. British journalist David Cohen, who has reported for such publications as the *Financial Times* and *The Independent*, writes in his excellent book *Chasing the Red, White, and Blue* that he was shocked to find stark inequality in the United States, not to mention poverty: 40 percent of America's children live below or near poverty level. (And the official definition of poverty—an annual income of $16,400 for a family of four—is a miserly one.) In 1999 and 2000, Cohen spent months retracing parts of Tocqueville's 1831 journey across the United States, comparing then and now. What makes his book audacious is that he dares to contradict the Frenchman. As right as Tocqueville was about so much, Cohen argues, his assertion that in America "equality is something fated . . . universal and permanent" has been proven wrong. Interviews with people from many walks of life and extensive background research led Cohen to argue that inequality in the United States is harsh and getting worse, but neither the nation's leaders nor its citizens care enough to combat it. The economic boom of the 1990s created unprecedented budget surpluses at state and federal levels, he notes, suggesting that "Americans have the economic means to help the least-well-off members of their society, but not the will to do so."

RONALD REAGAN AND
THE TRIUMPH OF WEALTH

Although we Americans don't often talk about it, there is no great mystery about the source of our rising inequality. Our government has been dominated for the past twenty years by people and policies that favor the well-to-do over everyone else. With Republicans leading the way but Democrats close behind, America's lawmakers have showered tax cuts on the wealthy even as they cut spending for the poor; resisted meaningful increases in the minimum wage while shoveling trillions of dollars in military contracts to corporations, some of which have repeatedly been caught charging such ridiculously inflated prices as $409 for a $39 household sink; helped drive down working- and middle-class wages by encouraging so-called free-trade deals that send jobs overseas; encouraged the corporate megamergers that bring layoffs and price increases; and relaxed or eliminated regulations designed to protect the public from the kind of corporate fraud and greed exposed during the Enron scandal.

Enron, whose 2001 bankruptcy was the largest in world history, exemplified how biased America's economic and political systems are in favor of the rich versus the poor. When Enron collapsed, its workers and average stockholders lost an estimated $25 to $50 billion worth of pension funds and share value because neither the company nor its auditors, the Arthur Andersen company, told the truth about Enron's perilous condition. Company executives, however, cashed out early, walking away with hundreds of millions of dollars. Enron stole another $50 billion by manipulating California's electricity market to create phony shortages and drive up prices. It bilked the nation's taxpayers, too. Because Clinton-era deregulation allowed it to transfer assets to foreign tax shelters, Enron paid no federal income tax in four of the five years before its bankruptcy; the rest of us had to make up the shortfall. And Enron is no isolated case. In 1995 alone, thousands of America's biggest corporations paid no income taxes, according to *The Cheating of America*, a devastating exposé by Charles Lewis, Bill Allison, and the Center for Public Integrity that estimates that corporations and the wealthy evade $195 billion a year in tax obligations.

The triumph of wealth over wisdom and markets over

morality dates to the election of Ronald Reagan as president in 1980; the increase in inequality correlates closely with his ascension to power. In the thirteen years before Reagan's presidency, according to United States Census Bureau data, the poorest one-fifth of all households increased their share of national income by 6.5 percent, while the wealthiest one-fifth's share fell by nearly 10 percent. This trend reflected in part the Great Society programs passed under President Lyndon Johnson in the 1960s, which increased access to food, health care, and equal opportunity for the nation's poor people. In the 1980s, however, the pendulum shifted back toward inequality: the share of national income going to the poorest one-fifth of Americans fell by 11.6 percent while the wealthiest one-fifth gained nearly 20 percent. This reversal was not caused solely by Reagan's policies. Increasing integration of the world economy left American manufacturing vulnerable to low-wage competition from overseas, which in turn gave American firms greater leverage to drive down wages at home with threats to relocate abroad. But Reagan did nothing to counter these trends or mitigate their consequences. On the contrary, he declared that any government intervention with market forces was misguided and counterproductive.

Drawing on the nation's Calvinist roots, Reagan especially disparaged federal assistance to the poor as a wasteful, destructive form of socialism that encouraged immoral behavior. One of the stories he loved to tell featured a so-called welfare queen, a woman who supposedly drove her Cadillac to the grocery store, used federally supplied food stamps to buy oranges and a bottle of vodka, and drove off happily to get drunk. When reporters inquired, neither Reagan nor his aides could supply the woman's name or any other corroborating evidence. But Reagan never let the facts get in the way of a good story, especially one that served his political purposes. He had an unshakable ability to believe what he wanted to believe: that the apartheid government in South Africa eliminated segregation, that the Russian language has no word for freedom, that he himself never traded arms for hostages in the Iran-contra scandal.

Ronald Reagan's two terms as president ended in 1989; in the mid-1990s, he drifted into the uncomprehending netherworld of Alzheimer's disease. As I write, in July 2002, Mr. Reagan is said to be so close to death that he may have passed away by the time these words are published. But living or dead, he remains the most influential politician in America today, the man whose anti-government, pro-business ideology still shapes the assumptions and policies that reign in official Washington. Indeed, Reagan may as well still be president, for all that the country has departed from his vision since he left office, especially in the domestic sphere. In 2001 George W. Bush's first major initiative as president directly copied the centerpiece of Reagan's economic strategy—a large tax cut whose benefits flowed overwhelmingly to the nation's wealthiest citizens. Even more telling is how Bill Clinton, though nominally a Democrat, spent his two terms as president limiting social spending, deregulating corporations, cracking down on welfare, and generally governing like a Republican (as Republicans themselves jealously admitted). Beyond his own opportunism, the reason for Clinton's abandonment of his party's traditional principles is that, as explained below, Reagan's legacy left him little choice.

Reagan was certainly the most important president of the past thirty years, and arguably the most important since Franklin Roosevelt. Just as Roosevelt inaugurated a new era in American history in the 1930s with New Deal programs that established a limited welfare state, so Reagan brought that era to a close by attacking the welfare state and putting the market back in charge. He began by crippling specific programs with spending cuts, but his larger achievement was ideological: he discredited the very idea that government should intervene in the economy to assist the poor and disadvantaged, regulate corporate conduct, or otherwise pursue a vision of the public interest that diverged from unrestrained private enterprise. Reagan championed a version of capitalism where the government's role in smoothing over the market's rough edges—by providing food stamps, protecting the right of workers to organize for better treatment, preventing corporations from cheating customers and investors or polluting the environment—was sharply reduced. He insisted that government is the cause of society's ills and markets the solution; leave the market alone, and everyone will end up better off. Although this view began to face fresh questioning thanks to the Enron scandal, it continues to dominate public discussion and policymaking in the United States. The man himself may be gone, but we still live in the Reagan era.

The victories that established his dominance over American politics were won during his first six months in office. In the name of less government, he cut virtually all forms of spending—including unemployment benefits, job training, food stamps, child nutrition, and subsidized housing—that served poor and working-class Americans. He vastly increased military spending—limited government did not apply in the face of the Soviet menace, he explained—mandating increases that within four years doubled the Pentagon's funding, to nearly $300 billion a year. Finally, he reduced taxes by 10 percent for all income levels. Describing the cuts as "across-the-board" made them sound fair, but they amounted to an incredible windfall for the wealthy, whose larger incomes meant larger tax reductions. Meanwhile, the effective corporate tax rate dropped from 33 to 16 percent and depreciation rules were made so generous that many corporations, including Reagan's old employer, General Electric, ended up paying no income tax at all—or even receiving rebates.

The tax cuts were an unwitting stroke of genius on Reagan's part, for they locked in his domestic priorities for years to come. How? Because they drained the United States Treasury, thus leaving Reagan's successors unable to restore social spending even if they wanted to. It credits Reagan with too much Machiavellian cunning to believe that he intended this outcome, as some critics charged; more likely is that he truly believed his "supply-side" tax cuts would unleash a torrent of new investment from the rich and corporate sources. Instead, however, the money was spent on the financial speculation and conspicuous consumption that defined the gaudy 1980s—there were four times as many corporate mergers as in the 1970s—while the lost revenues led to the biggest federal budget deficits in American history. With the government so deeply in debt, any efforts to restore social spending faced an impossible uphill battle; for the rest of Reagan's presidency, Democrats in Congress mainly sought to block further cuts. Of course, Democrats could have found funds by scaling back military spending and the tax cuts, but Reagan wouldn't hear of it, and because of his popularity the Democrats were afraid to propose it.

By the time Reagan left office in 1989, the deficit had grown so large that the Republican-dominated bond markets were demanding action, leading George Bush to break a campaign promise and raise taxes, dooming his reelection chances in 1992. Bill Clinton continued the deficit reduction fight while complaining privately that it made him look like Herbert Hoover, the Republican president whose tight fiscal policies had helped bring on the Great Depression. Clinton's one ambitious social proposal was to bring national health care to the United States, an initiative fatally compromised by, among other things, his fear of challenging Reagan-era dogma about the sanctity of private enterprise; insurance companies, not the government, would have run Clinton's health care system. Otherwise, Clinton in his first term enacted none of the jobs, education, or other social programs one would expect from a Democrat except an expansion of the earned income tax credit, which ended up reducing the taxes of working-poor families who had children by an average of $540 a year.

In 1995 Clinton made his embrace of Reagan's ideological legacy official, declaring, "The era of big government is over." Later that year, he demonstrated a spasm of courage, defying the Gingrich Republicans who insisted on shutting down the government in a fight over the federal budget. But facing re-election in 1996, he implicitly endorsed Reagan's perspective on poor people as undeserving freeloaders by signing a welfare "reform" bill that would force millions of mothers into the workforce, even if they could not afford day care for their children. In his second term, he continued to embrace Reagan priorities both with tax cuts biased toward the wealthy and with aggressive corporate deregulation. His enforcement of anti-trust laws was even laxer than Reagan's; he stood by as more and more sectors of the economy came under the control of fewer and fewer corporations. Education was the one area where Clinton did deliver for working-class voters, passing tax credits that helped some ten million Americans go to college. Meanwhile, he took great pride in the number of jobs being created in America but ignored the fact that one-fourth of them paid poverty wages. He rebuffed suggestions that he fight for a significant raise in the minimum wage.

Like Reagan in the 1980s, Clinton in the 1990s presided over what were celebrated as good economic times. And the economy did grow under Clinton: the high-tech boom was real, the efficiencies it spread throughout the economy raised productivity and created wealth, and some of that wealth trickled down to average working people. But most was captured by the well-off; the sparkling aggregate growth figures masked a further widening of the gap between rich and poor. "The '90s have seen a greater polarization of income in the U.S. than at any point since the end of World War II," wrote *Business Week.* The stock market now drove the economy rather than vice versa, leading corporations to "downsize," shedding workers and cutting costs to impress Wall Street analysts. Even workers lucky enough to keep their jobs often saw them restructured to part-time positions that included no health care or pension benefits. For millions of the working poor, a steady paycheck was no guarantee of a decent life. Hunger stalked the poorest citizens of the world's biggest food-producing nation. By 2001 some thirty-one million Americans—nearly one in every nine citizens—were unsure of where their next meal was coming from.

Alas, inequality is poised to deepen in the years ahead, both because the Bush administration and Congress continue to favor the wealthy in their tax and spending policies and because the United States economy is no longer creating enough well-paying jobs to support a stable middle class. Nearly half of the tax reductions that Washington ordered in early 2001 will go to the top 4 percent of income earners; only 14.7 percent of the cuts will benefit the bottom 60 percent of Americans. Meanwhile, corporate crime—the insider trading, deception, and theft practiced by Enron and who knows how many other big companies—has shrunk millions of Americans' savings and retirement nest eggs to the vanishing point.

As for working one's way out of poverty, good luck. Citing data from the United States Bureau of Labor Statistics, David Cohen reports that 46 percent of the jobs with the most projected growth in America to the year 2005—jobs such as janitor, retail clerk, and waiter or waitress—pay poverty wages. Many workers will choose to work a second or third job to provide for their families—an increasingly common strategy for Americans trying to retain their middle-class dreams or identities, but one which leaves families even less time together. More poverty and inequality, it seems, will be accompanied by more stress and isolation.

THE INVISIBILITY OF CLASS

America is more economically unequal today than at any time since the Great Depression of 1929, and one of the most disturbing aspects of the problem is that we as a society barely acknowledge it, much less talk about how to respond. In Europe and Japan, even minor increases in economic inequality attract extensive media coverage and provoke discussion among politicians, clergy, and other opinion leaders, because those elites recognize the attendant dangers. By contrast, the elites who dominate America's political, economic, and media systems carry on as if all is well, which it is for them. But only, I would argue, in the short term.

As disturbing as widespread poverty amid plenty is, the shrinking of the middle class is the most ominous aspect of

America's growing inequality. Throughout modern world history, it has been a secure middle class—and the belief by lower classes that they could rise to enter that class—that has kept nations politically stable and socially peaceful. The corporate and right-wing forces behind rising inequality in the United States are therefore playing with fire. But they are blinded by their ideology of "market fundamentalism," to borrow financier George Soros's term, an ideology as rigid and all-encompassing as the Islamic fundamentalism they often condemn.

We Americans cannot successfully confront our economic problems until we can talk honestly about the economic system in which we live. Unfortunately, it has long been impossible for Americans to discuss capitalism in anything but the most worshipful tones; doing otherwise gets one branded as a radical and ejected from mainstream debate. See, for example, journalist Naomi Klein's critical examination of corporate globalization in *No Logo*, a runaway best-seller in Great Britain and her native Canada that was not even reviewed by leading newspapers and magazines in the United States.

Likewise, social class is a much-discussed fact of life in Britain and other advanced capitalist nations but a forbidden subject among Americans. Our elites dislike the topic for obvious reasons, and the rest of us have been socialized into thinking it simply doesn't exist. The only time the phrase "class warfare" appears in our media is when it is invoked against such proposals as requiring corporations and the wealthy to pay higher taxes. Cutting social welfare spending, expanding high-end tax breaks, firing workers by the thousands—somehow these attacks against America's nonaffluent majority are never described as "class warfare."

"America is a very segregated place, and it's not only segregated by race, it's also segregated by class," Andy Kolker, the codirector of the documentary *People Like Us*, said on the Washington, D.C.–area television show *The Coffee House*. "We don't talk about that in this country because of our belief that we're really all kind of middle class. We're all Americans together." Our egalitarian roots contribute to this myopia. Because of our past, when class relations were more equal, we want to believe that class is irrelevant. The truth, as people around the world well know, is that one's class decisively shapes one's life, especially one's economic prospects.

"For the vast majority of Americans, the most important determinant of their success, or lack of it, is the situation they are born into and the opportunity it affords," Jack Litzenberg, the director of the Pathways Out of Poverty program at the Mott Foundation in Detroit, told David Cohen. "Equality is a myth. Social mobility is increasingly a myth. The American Dream is a myth. But we hold on to these myths and they define who we are."

The Cold War ended in 1989. Are Americans at last ready to recognize both the pluses and minuses of capitalism, rather than wallow in the hagiography that has characterized most of our discourse about free enterprise? Capitalism has much to recommend it: it is unsurpassed at producing goods, spurring innovation, and generating wealth, as America's history shows. The greed and competition that make the system go, however, tend to enhance social inequality, and the market's inability to value social assets like clean air and water often leads to environmental degradation. These negative consequences explain why even staunchly pro-capitalist economists have historically advocated a mediating role for government: only government has the power to keep the market's strengths and weaknesses in balance and assure a level playing field for all members of the society—by providing a legal framework, business regulations, tax and fiscal policy, social welfare programs, and the like. Where a given nation draws the line in the trade-off between economic efficiency and social felicity is a matter of choice. One reason the welfare state in America is so limited is the strong strain of libertarianism that has always informed our approach to capitalism. Americans want the freedom to grab as much money as we can, and we don't begrudge others the same opportunity. But it's a dog-eat-dog system, and that makes other people the competition; if they fall behind, that's their problem. By contrast, virtually all of the capitalist nations of Europe and Asia have opted for a stronger state role in channeling capitalism's energies and moderating its excesses. Only the United States, for example, lacks a national health care system. America's less extensive welfare state also helps explain why the streets of nearly all of our major cities are blighted by homeless people, a sight that largely disappears when one travels to continental Europe or Japan. Because the capitalist nations of Europe and Asia spend more on public health, education, and jobs programs, social mobility for their poor and working classes is now higher than it is in the United States. These nations may sacrifice some economic growth in return for greater equality, and their unemployment rates may be higher, but poverty levels are lower and social cohesion greater.

The inequality that overcame the United States in the 1980s and 1990s was a direct result of public policies that gave market forces priority over all other social values; it follows, therefore, that this inequality could be reduced by reorienting government's role within American capitalism. This may sound quixotic to American ears, because our culture has been saturated by market fundamentalism for so many years. But talk specifics and it turns out that a majority of Americans do favor raising the minimum wage, do want the Social Security program maintained, do approve of government intervention against downsizing and other corporate tactics that put the profits of the wealthy few above the good of the broader community.

If we Americans want the American Dream to become real again, we will have to challenge the market fundamentalism that currently reigns throughout our land, starting with our elected representatives in Washington. Turning lawmakers away from an ideology that has rewarded them with power and campaign funds won't be easy, but the times are plainly ripe for change. The recent corporate scandals make clear the dangers of unregulated capitalism, and the abundant evidence that George W. Bush, Dick Cheney, and other senior administration officials have fabulously profited from the same shady business practices they now denounce makes it harder for them to block genuine reform. Achieving economic justice in America is an imposing challenge, but no more imposing than the Wizard of Oz's command that Dorothy and her compatriots bring him the broomstick of the Wicked Witch of the West. If we can recall the lessons of our national fairy tale—believe in yourself, stick by your friends, and fight for what's right—perhaps we may win that most American of prizes: a happy ending.

8

THE TRAGEDY OF AMERICAN DEMOCRACY

The old German was giving Arturo a language lesson when I walked up to ask about renting a bicycle. They were sitting in the shade near the entrance to a hotel in the countryside about an hour outside Havana. The old German was listening patiently, encouragingly, as Arturo struggled to express himself in the language of Goethe. Arturo's accent was pretty atrocious but his grammar was solid, down to having mastered the rule of putting the verb at the end of the sentence. Not bad for a guy learning German on his own, out of a book.

"Er spricht ja gut," I called out. Arturo blushed to hear me praise his efforts. The old German agreed, but as we chatted, he could tell from my own accent that I was no German. He asked where I was from, and when I replied, he instantly shot back, "So, do you have a new president yet?"

It was November 12, 2000. The United States presidential election had taken place five days before, and still it was unclear whether George W. Bush or Al Gore was the winner. I had found no Western newspapers in Cuba, but I was watching CNN obsessively in the hotels where it was available.

With each passing day, a definitive outcome seemed more and more elusive.

"They still don't know," I replied. "It depends which man wins Florida, and the vote there is a mess."

Seeing that Arturo was having trouble following the conversation in German, the old man switched to English. "But this is unbelievable!" he exclaimed. "The United States has the modern technology. How can you not know?" A note of reprimand crept into his voice as he added, "We too want to know who will be president. We too must live with his decisions."

"Is it true that Bush's brother runs the government of Florida?" Arturo interjected.

"Yes, he's the governor."

"So Bush will win Florida, no?"

"Well, it's not supposed to work like that," I said. "But maybe."

"But of course Bush will win," said Arturo. "His brother cannot let him lose. I heard on the news that Al Gore won the most votes across the country, but if he loses Florida, Bush becomes president. Is that really true?"

"Yes," I said. "It's complicated." I sighed, thinking about how to explain the intricacies of the Electoral College. A mischievous smile brightened Arturo's face.

"It sounds like you are having trouble with your democracy in the United States," he said. "Perhaps Cuba should send you election observers next time."

I had read that joke a couple of days before in *La Prensa*, the Communist Party newspaper of Cuba, but Arturo delivered it well, and I smiled ruefully. But the old German found the line hilariously funny. "Yes, good idea," he chortled, his potbelly shaking. "Cuba must help the United States with democracy. Election observers. Very good idea."

American presidential elections are always big news overseas, but never had one captured the world's attention quite like this. The 2000 contest—or, more accurately, its ignoble Florida aftermath—not only gave foreigners a good laugh at America's expense, it provided a drama whose daily twists and turns were as captivating as any soap opera.

"I followed it very closely," Michiel Lingeman, a thirty-six-year-old auto industry executive in Amsterdam, later told me, smiling at the memory. "I really enjoyed it. I was reading the newspapers every day, watching the news, checking on the Internet to learn the latest developments. You never knew what would happen next. Who is ahead today? Who is going to court? What will the judges say this time? At my company, I would say that your election was what everyone talked about during the lunch break for at least two weeks."

Foreigners had an advantage in trying to make sense of the election. Their distance from the event made it easier to see the forest for the trees. Their partisan passions were less engaged and their national pride not at stake; they felt free to laugh at the absurdities. When South Americans or Europeans heard that Al Gore had received approximately 500,000 more votes nationwide than George Bush had, they wondered what kind of democracy it was that ignored majority rule. When foreign journalists reported that Florida's governor was Bush's brother and its top election official had co-chaired his campaign in Florida, they did not feel obliged to adopt the neutral tone of American news coverage; their strong implication was that the fix was in. That implication intensified when the Republican-dominated United States Supreme Court voted 5 to 4 to halt a recount of ballots in Florida, assuring Bush's victory. "A pall of illegitimacy hangs over Bush's inaugural," opined the *Hindustan Times* of India.

If it came as a shock for foreigners to see the world's proudest democracy fumbling its most basic political ritual, the shock was not entirely unpleasant. For years, America's self-righteousness had grated on foreign ears. Washington's insistence that it alone was the arbiter of proper democratic procedure had long forced other nations to obey Washington's commands—and remain silent about its double standards—in order to stay on the empire's good side. Now, the humiliation in Florida was giving the boastful bully his comeuppance. The *Mail & Guardian* of South Africa editorialized, with tongue in cheek, "It is a shameful reflection on our continent that, in their hour of need, we were not there beside our American brothers and sisters to help and advise where we could, in the same way as they do when our elections come around. . . . Before the onset of the contest itself, we should have set up seminars in the main rural centers, where the various models of democracy would have been explained, including the detail that it is 'the people' who are meant to rule and not 'the Electoral College.' "

Thus the 2000 election gave rise to one more embarrassing fact about the United States that Americans don't talk about but foreigners know perfectly well: the man now occupying the Oval Office was not elected president. George W. Bush was appointed president, yes, but only after a tragicomedy of errors that made the United States a global laughingstock and stripped the result of any respectability. Yet even foreigners often do not grasp just how corrupt the election was; there was more to the scandal than confusingly designed ballots and America's tendency to reduce matters of principle to lawsuit technicalities. At the time, events were unfolding in such a rapid-fire, disorienting way that even the best journalism could not achieve the perspective needed to convey the full story. Now the dust has settled, and information has emerged that was unknown or overlooked during the crisis itself. For example, Patrick Buchanan, the right-wing candidate, has admitted—to deafening indifference on the part of the American news media—that an honest count of the votes awarded to him in Florida would have given those votes, and thus the presidency, to Al Gore.

Was the 2000 election merely a joke? Or was it also a crime? Some of the failures that marred the election's integrity were mechanical (bad voting machines), some were procedural (the media's race to name a winner before all the votes were counted), but the greatest failures were legal and moral. The proof is not definitive, but there is considerable evidence that the vote in Florida was, in effect, stolen by the Bush campaign. Equally disturbing is the *way* it appears to have been stolen: through official efforts to deprive black citizens of their right to vote. Less than forty years ago, American blacks were being beaten bloody for peacefully marching to win the right to vote. If their rights were indeed violated by Florida state officials in alliance with the Bush campaign, it is a shameful sign that the United States has still not overcome the legacy of racism that dates to our nation's founding.

It's understandable that Americans might want to avoid looking the election of 2000 squarely in the face. What's done is done, George W. Bush is president, and in a time of war, unity behind the commander in chief is essential. Yet it is dangerous to ignore the truth about something as important as a presidential election, especially since the lessons of this election illuminate a deeper crisis in our political system. The full story of Election 2000 reveals how constrained voters' freedom of choice really is in the United States; how poorly served we are by the mainstream media; how lopsided our ideological playing field is—we have a rabid right wing, two centrist parties, and no real left wing; how tightly the process is controlled by an entrenched governing class of incumbent politicians and wealthy financiers—in short, how compromised and inconsistent our practice of democracy often is. To paraphrase Shakespeare, Election 2000 suggests that there is something rotten not only in the state of Florida but throughout our beloved republic. And before the problem can be fixed, it must be faced.

JEWS FOR BUCHANAN

It's hard for Americans to grasp what really happened during Election 2000, because the media that are supposed to inform us were themselves a big part of the problem. Their errors were a good example of what can happen when corporate ownership elevates profit-making and political conformity over civic responsibility and professional standards. On Election Night, the television networks humiliated themselves by naming first Gore, then no one, then Bush the winner of Florida. They united behind Bush only after the Fox News Network named him president-elect at 2:16 a.m. the next morning. Fox is a stridently right-wing network whose election unit was headed by John Ellis, Bush's cousin, and it based its judgment on an analysis of exit polls that proved unreliable. But the other TV networks were unable to independently check the analysis because years of cost-cutting had left them without enough reporters on the ground in Florida, so they eagerly seconded Fox's announcement.

The political significance of the networks' rush to judgment was enormous, for it created the crucial impression that

Bush had won the election and Gore was the sore loser demanding a recount. For the rest of the thirty-six-day crisis, the Bush campaign exploited this impression to claim that a recount was somehow cheating. This effort was helped immeasurably by Katherine Harris, the Bush campaign's co-chair in Florida, who as secretary of state repeatedly refused to authorize a full recount (or to step aside in recognition of her obvious conflict of interest). Far from puncturing the Bush campaign's anti-democratic posturing, the news media reinforced it, repeating the campaign's nonsensical claim that counting ballots by hand yielded inaccurate results and urging Gore to concede or risk damaging the nation's stability.

Recounting votes became an issue the day after the election, when elderly Jewish residents of Palm Beach County learned that their precinct of liberal Democrats had given right-winger Pat Buchanan his highest vote total in the state. They complained that the so-called butterfly ballot had been confusing. In an interview months later for John Nichols's indispensable book on the Florida debacle, *Jews for Buchanan*, Buchanan agreed. It was clear, he said, that "more Gore voters went to the polls than Bush voters on November 7 in Florida. If the results had reflected the actual sentiments of the people who voted, Al Gore would have won Florida, which means he would have had the majority in the electoral college and that he would be president today."

Had Buchanan forcefully argued this point at the time, American political history might be different: the idea that Al Gore was the cheated rather than the cheater might have become the assumption of media coverage, and steps might have been taken to rectify the mistaken count in Palm Beach County. The number of votes at issue was approximately

8,000—dwarfing Bush's 537-vote victory margin. And Buchanan did try, once, to set the record straight. Two days after
the election, he appeared on national television and was
honest enough to say that most of the Palm Beach County
votes did not belong to him. But fellow Republicans launched
a ferocious attack on his supposed disloyalty, and he soon
shut up.

And then there was race. Blacks encountered discrimination in Florida that dramatically lowered their vote totals. According to Allan J. Lichtman, a professor at American University in Washington, D.C., who analyzed the Florida vote
for the United States Commission on Civil Rights, "about one
in every seven or eight African-Americans statewide who
showed up for Florida's presidential election had their ballots
set aside as invalid." This rejection rate was 10 percent higher
than for whites, Lichtman notes, even when controlling for
differences in education, income, and first-time voting. Had
the two races been treated equally, he adds, "more than
60,000 additional ballots cast by blacks would have been
counted in the election." Since 93 percent of recorded votes
by blacks in Florida went to Al Gore, it follows that Gore
would have received about 54,000 extra votes, giving him a
clear victory over Bush.

Fewer black votes were counted partly because black (and
poor) precincts tended to have antiquated voting machines
that malfunctioned more often. A more disturbing problem is
that blacks appear to have been targeted by Florida officials
for removal from state voter lists before the election took
place. As revealed by British journalist Gregory Palast, the administration of Florida governor Jeb Bush pursued a very
aggressive purging of the state's voter rolls in 1999 and
2000. In theory, this was a legal operation to remove the

names of voters who had died, were double-listed, or were convicted felons. In practice, it disenfranchised thousands of blacks who had every legal right to vote. (It's worth noting that Palast revealed this information during the recount crisis in the newspaper *The Observer* and on BBC television but couldn't get it published in the United States until eight months later.)

And there was further racial discrimination. Many blacks later testified that they were turned away from voting by officials who claimed their names were not on the list. Stacy Powers, a radio reporter in Tampa who spent Election Day observing various polling places, estimated that "thousands" were turned away. There were also reports of physical intimidation, of police setting up roadblocks and harassing blacks on their way to the polls.

Such strong-arm tactics had been common across the American South in the pre–civil rights era. For example, in 1964 an aggressive white lawyer bullied numerous nonwhite citizens attempting to vote in Phoenix, Arizona, according to witnesses later interviewed by the *Pittsburgh Post-Gazette*. One witness, Lito Pena, who subsequently served thirty years in the Arizona legislature, recalled how the white lawyer demanded that nonwhites answer many personal questions and prove their command of English by interpreting a passage from the United States Constitution before being allowed to vote. The white lawyer's name was William Rehnquist.

Thirty-six years later, Rehnquist was the chief justice of the United States Supreme Court whose 5–4 decision prohibited recounting the votes in Florida. He was not alone in approaching the case with bias. Justices Clarence Thomas and Antonin Scalia had direct conflicts of interest. Thomas's wife was a consultant to the Bush campaign; Scalia had two sons working for law firms that represented Bush in the legal fight in Florida. Nevertheless, these justices did not remove themselves from the case. Instead, they joined the narrow majority in a ruling that was almost universally condemned as a partisan, intellectually shoddy intervention in the political process. The tenor of the ruling is revealed by Scalia's explanation for why a recount was unacceptable: a recount might "cast a cloud upon what [Bush] claims to be the legitimacy of his election"—as if Bush's mere claim to deserve the presidency were enough to settle the issue.

But all's well that ends well. At least that was the American media's final take on the 2000 election. A year after the fact, a consortium of major newspapers and professional statisticians who had analyzed all the uncounted votes in Florida announced its conclusions. The story made page one headlines across the country with the news that the Supreme Court, to quote the *New York Times*, "did not cast the deciding vote" after all: had the Court not halted the recount, Bush still would have narrowly won the election. Only careful readers of the accompanying news stories might realize that this conclusion unfairly interpreted the evidence. The recount the *Times* mentioned would have included only 60,000 of the 175,010 uncounted votes in Florida. It would have excluded "overvotes"—including the nearly 8,000 butterfly ballot votes Gore lost to Buchanan in Palm Beach County and 7,000 similarly mistaken ballots in Duval County—on the grounds that ballots containing two choices could not be given to any candidate. The disproportionate rejection of black votes was noted (though not the discriminatory practices that gave rise to it), but only in articles buried inside the newspapers. The overall message of the reporting, which appeared two months after the September 11 attacks, was that the right man had ended up in the White House after all.

"IS THERE *ANY* DIFFERENCE BETWEEN YOU?"

Lost in all the drama over who won Florida was the fact that most Americans didn't want either Bush or Gore to be president. Only 51 percent of the nation's eligible voters bothered to cast ballots in 2000, and since Buchanan and Ralph Nader won 3 percent of the vote between them, Bush and Gore were each left with support from only one-quarter of the electorate. This has become common in modern America. Bill Clinton gained reelection in 1996 on the strength of votes from only 24 percent of the electorate. Reagan drew only 27 percent in 1980, though the media declared he had won a "landslide" and a "mandate" because he had trounced Carter in the Electoral College. But do such terms as "landslide" and "mandate," with their implication of massive popular approval, really apply when half of the electorate declines to vote?

What does it say about American democracy that so many of our citizens consistently choose not to participate in selecting the nation's leaders? Our voter turnout levels are consistently lower than those of most other advanced capitalist democracies. In a measure of all elections between 1945 and 1998, the United States ranks 114th in the world in voter turnout, with only 48.3 percent of our electorate going to the polls. Italy ranks first, with 92.5 percent. Belgium, Holland, Sweden, New Zealand, Australia, and Germany are all in the 80s, while Spain has averaged 77 percent, the United Kingdom 74.9 percent, Japan 69 percent, France 67 percent, and India 61 percent.

It's easy, and correct, to say that everyone should vote; in a democracy, citizenship carries responsibilities as well as rights. But it's also easy to see why many Americans don't: there is little real choice among candidates and the political process seems irretrievably remote from our own lives—a squalid yet boring spectacle conducted by and for the political elite in Washington, the media jackals who cover them, and the wealthy interests who finance the whole thing.

Jim Hightower, the Texas populist, satirized the sorry state of American democracy in the title of his recent book *If the Gods Had Meant Us to Vote They Would Have Given Us Candidates.* The truth is, it's hard to tell most candidates apart in the United States; whether Democrat or Republican, they usually differ little on issues but compensate with rhetorical support for "working families" or "compassionate conservatism" or whatever catchphrase their handlers have tested on focus groups. Meanwhile, the media, the source of most voters' information about the candidates, are obsessed with process and personality—Who's ahead? What is the candidate *really* like?—but presume that substantive issues are dull money-losers, and so present them that way. Local television no longer covers election campaigns at all except to run thirty-second attack ads by candidates that insult the truth but make the stations piles of money ($500 million during the congressional elections of 1998). The astronomical price of the ads is the main reason campaigns cost so much, which in turn explains why candidates spend most of their time begging wealthy sponsors for money rather than speaking with actual voters. Considering how voters are ignored, patronized, manipulated, and lied to during elections, it's a wonder even half of the American electorate shows up to vote.

Before the Florida debacle injected some drama into it, the choice between Al Gore and George W. Bush was widely ridiculed as the most uninspiring in years. Ralph Nader exaggerated when he said there was no difference between Bush and Gore; the two diverged significantly on abortion, gun control, and the environment. But Nader's basic point was right, especially on economic issues. The candidates proved it themselves during the second debate of the 2000 campaign. In response after response, Bush and Gore sounded so similar that finally the interviewer, public television's normally mild-mannered Jim Lehrer, asked in exasperation, "Is there *any* difference between you?" Of course, Bush and Gore were appealing to so-called swing voters that night and so hewed even closer to the center than usual. But they did not greatly differ during the rest of the campaign either, and one reason why is that they relied on the same moneyed elite to finance their campaigns. (Bush raised $191 million for the 2000 campaign, more than any candidate in history. Gore made do with a mere $133 million.)

The ability to raise money is now the single most important qualification for running for high office in the United States. Long before actual voters get a chance to choose among candidates in primary elections, those candidates must succeed in what has been called the "wealth primary"—the race to prove one's fund-raising clout. Without it, the media do not take a candidate's chances seriously and so withhold the coverage needed to make him or her known to voters. Of course, to raise a war chest, a candidate must convince potential donors that he or she deserves their support. This fact gives an enormous amount of political power to the nation's richest individuals. The richest 4 percent of the population provide nearly 100 percent of all individual campaign contributions. These people are not monolithic in their views, but they tend to support policies that will preserve their privileges, such as high-end tax breaks and a corporate-friendly approach to government regulation. Nonindividual contributions come from labor unions and corporations. Since corporations' contributions outnumber labor's by seven to one, the well-off maintain an overwhelming advantage.

Under such conditions, is it any wonder that most candidates refrain from taking positions that might displease the donor class? Like Republicans and Democrats in general, Bush's and Gore's economic positions were friendlier to corporations and the well-to-do than to the bottom 80 percent of the population. Neither candidate criticized corporate welfare subsidies that drain hundreds of billions of dollars from the federal treasury every year, especially through a military budget riddled with absurd cost overruns. (Pentagon workers, for example, have bought prostitutes for themselves and paid for breast enhancement for their girlfriends.) Both men supported the World Trade Organization and other mechanisms of so-called free trade that raise profits for corporations but bring workers unemployment and lower wages. Judging by their silence, both also found the idea of raising the minimum wage as unthinkable as making corporations and the wealthy pay their fair share of taxes.

The corruption of the current system infects Congress as well as the White House and Democrats as well as Republicans. Bill Clinton was the king of raising "soft money," so named because, unlike "hard money," it was tax-deductible. As was clear to everyone but his own attorney general, Clinton, with help from Gore, repeatedly broke the law with White House coffee fund-raisers and Lincoln Bedroom sleepovers. Yet it is Republicans who have resisted campaign finance reform most fiercely, perhaps because they raise nearly twice as much money from the prevailing system as Democrats do. Proof of how pervasive the rot is came following the collapse of Enron, the energy company that was the single biggest contributor to George W. Bush's political career. Scheduling congressional hearings on the collapse proved awkward, for it was soon discovered that nearly every member of Congress serving on the relevant committees had taken donations from the firm.

Big money distorts American democracy in another way as well: it reinforces the stranglehold that incumbent politicians exercise over elections. Donors prefer to give money to incumbents, because incumbents can more surely deliver returns on that investment by voting favorably, writing laws, prodding the bureaucracy, and the like. Congressional incumbents raise ten times more money than challengers, giving them a virtually insurmountable advantage at election time. Micah Sifry reports in *Spoiling for a Fight: Third-Party Politics in America* that in 2000, 98 percent of House of Representatives incumbents won reelection; in 1998, 99 percent won. "In recent years a House incumbent has been more likely to die in office than be beaten by a challenger from his own party," adds Sifry. The odds are stacked even less fairly at the state level; a majority of Americans live in what amount to one-party fiefdoms.

To complete the circle of corruption, incumbent politicians and the major parties write the rules for political competition that deprive challengers of an equal opportunity to defeat them. The practice of gerrymandering—carving up districts to decide which voters will vote for which incumbents—assures Democrats and Republicans alike of safe seats in much the same way that price-fixing corporations divide up customers to boost profits. No less self-serving was the Democrats' and Republicans' exclusion of Nader and Buchanan from the 2000 presidential debates. These nationally televised debates were most citizens' only sustained, unfiltered exposure to the candidates. Polls showed that most Americans wanted the minor-party candidates included, perhaps in hopes of forcing some zest and diversity into the discussion. Yet the Democrats' and Republicans' power play succeeded. The exclusion of Nader and Buchanan never even became a controversy, because the media agreed they didn't belong, and that was that.

WHY AMERICA HAS NO LEFT WING

There is nothing wrong with the United States having a political party that vigorously champions the interests of the well-to-do, but do we really need two of them? Broadening the debate would not only yield smarter policies by forcing each side to confront weaknesses in its position; it would also excite greater popular involvement in the political process. As it stands, voters face a choice between two parties with different names but increasingly similar economic and foreign policy philosophies. This system leaves the nonaffluent underrepresented, and probably discourages voter turnout as well.

Why is it that the United States, virtually alone among the wealthy capitalist democracies, has only two major parties? Part of the explanation dates back to the founders, who eschewed a parliamentary-dominant political system and mandated winner-take-all elections. Political parties didn't exist in America at the time, but the eventual effect of these choices was a structural bias against third parties. Because only the top vote-getter in any American election gains office, voters who choose third-party candidates risk wasting their votes. It's true that the Republicans started as a third party and, under Lincoln, rode the issue of slavery to majority status, but all other third-party efforts have collapsed (though not without sometimes forcing the major parties to address new issues). In the modern era, Democrats and Republicans routinely rig rules over access to ballots, media, and funding (see the debates example above) to thwart the emergence of third parties.

All of which also helps explain what, by world standards, is a strikingly odd feature of American politics: its lack of a left-wing party.

Michiel Lingeman, the Amsterdam auto executive, told me he voted for the most conservative of Holland's five major political parties, the VVD, the People's Party for Freedom and Democracy, "because it is the most pro-business." Yet he rooted for Al Gore while following America's election. "I think all Dutch people did," he said. "We are a foreign country, and Bush made it clear he did not care about foreign countries." But, I pointed out, Republicans are known as the pro-business party in the United States, not Democrats. "Well," said Michiel, "that is a funny thing about the United States. Both of your parties are more conservative than right-wing parties are here. Believe me, my party is the most pro-business in Holland, but it is to the left of Democrats in supporting regulation of the market, a sensible welfare state, and these kinds of things."

The lack of a left-wing party in the United States has deep historical roots. Organizing workers was difficult in a country whose vast abundance beckoned them away from cities to pursue fortunes on the frontier; where language barriers among immigrants and racial divisions between blacks and whites complicated worker solidarity; where the disadvantaged have often been unable to exercise the right to vote; and where a national identity of freedom and individualism rejected anything resembling the authoritarianism of Communism. In the 1960s, the New Left explicitly rejected Communism and grew influential enough to help stop the Vietnam War. But in the 1970s, the anti-war, civil rights, women's, and other elements of a potential left-wing movement, instead of uniting, fractured into self-absorbed proponents of identity politics. Meanwhile, Richard Nixon seized on the alienation some working-class whites felt from the counterculture to position the Republican Party as the champion of traditional American values: God, flag, and country. In the 1980s, Reagan perfected this strategy, consolidating the party's hold on the South, the Midwest, and the Mountain States. Although Reagan was never as popular as his public relations apparatus made him appear, intimidated Democrats assumed they had to move right to counter his appeal. The party nominated a Northern liberal for the last time in 1988, the hapless Michael Dukakis, before the party's corporate wing decisively vanquished the left and secured the nomination of Bill Clinton, a Southern moderate, in 1992.

Instead of a left, America has a right wing that has proven powerful enough to pull both major parties significantly in its direction over the past twenty years. Although Bill Clinton governed like a Republican in many respects, he was reviled by Christian fundamentalists as a draft-dodging, pot-smoking advocate of abortion, homosexuality, and socialism. They were determined to bring him down, and they had at their disposal a well-financed political machine. Besides grassroots strength, especially in the South, the right has its own daily newspaper in the political capital, the *Washington Times*, and another in the financial capital, the *New York Post*; and it controls the editorial page of the nation's largest paper, the *Wall Street Journal*. It owns television networks—both Christian and commercial, like Fox—as well as hundreds of radio stations. Together, this apparatus can focus popular outrage on Washington. This it did from the start of Clinton's presidency, accusing him of everything from financial corruption (in the Whitewater real estate deal), to the murder of aide Vince Foster, to fathering a child out of wedlock.

The right wing's influence over American politics was best illustrated by the episode that, even more than Election 2000, left foreigners shaking their heads in puzzled amusement: Clinton's impeachment. I was in Europe shortly after the story broke that the president's affair with White House intern Monica Lewinsky was provoking calls for his removal from office. In Paris, the reaction of Jean-Francis Held, a veteran journalist and founding editor of the newsweekly magazine *L'Événement du Jeudi*, was typical. Held loved to break investigative stories, but what was so scandalous about a politician having a mistress? "Tell me the president pulled big strings for a financial contributor and I am interested. But tell me he had an affair with a young woman on his staff? I am sorry, I am not interested." Foreigners like Held blamed the Lewinsky scandal on America's puritanical views about sex, which was true. But the scandal would not have blossomed into a serious constitutional crisis had not the right wing enjoyed such powerful influence within Congress, not just among religious Republicans but also among Democrats who feared the right wing's wrath come election time. To get Clinton impeached and nearly removed from office was, on purely tactical grounds, an impressive achievement, for the American public never shared the right's outrage or its conviction that Clinton should go. Many people found the president's behavior repugnant, the details of his affair disgusting, and his brazen lies about it outrageous. Nevertheless, they separated such matters from evaluation of his job performance, which was consistently high. Clinton survived impeachment when the Senate voted not to convict, but his reputation was forever tarnished. The right, meanwhile, went on in the next election to hijack the White House.

OF THE PEOPLE, BY THE PEOPLE, FOR THE PEOPLE?

The lack of genuine choice facing American voters is not as complete as that facing citizens of Cuba or China, but it is hardly what the Founding Fathers had in mind. How long the Republicrats' hold over American politics will continue is hard to guess: Our Constitution never mentions political parties, much less Democrats or Republicans, and as the two parties have moved closer to each other but further away from average citizens, their mass support has diminished. In 1999 a Gallup poll found that 38 percent of Americans considered themselves independent of Democrats and Republicans. And each of the last three presidential elections has featured significant third-party challenges, despite the imposing obstacles to third parties in the American system. For the moment, the major parties cling to power through a combination of big-money support, underhanded maneuvering, and sheer inertia. Nevertheless, their patrons in the moneyed elite seem supremely confident. When President Bush, seeking to distance himself from Enron, told a crowd of Republican donors in February 2002 that he hoped to encourage greater corporate responsibility, the audience assumed he had to be joking and literally laughed in his face.

But what of the American people? Will we yield to disgust and retreat further into political disengagement? Or will we fight to restore fairness and fiber to our democracy?

Loosening the grip of big money is an obvious necessity, and the passage of the McCain-Feingold campaign finance law in early 2002 was a hopeful sign. Yet even McCain-Feingold is only a small step forward. It bans "soft money" but doubles the amount of "hard money" a person can contribute, thus boosting the clout of the nation's richest donors. This trade-off, supporters said, was the price of getting the bill through Congress—clear proof that resistance to reform remains strong among incumbents of both parties. A more thoroughgoing solution would be to implement public financing of elections. Maine and Arizona have passed public financing laws—Arizona even had the pluck to fund its law with a tax on lobbyists—and the results have been inspiring: a greater diversity of candidates, higher voter turnout, less control of the process by the monied few. Elections also would cost much less in the first place if Americans remembered that the airwaves belong to us and insisted that radio and television stations provide ample coverage of candidates and debates, rather than extorting $500 million in advertising fees every year. Finally, instant runoff voting, which San Francisco recently adopted, would undermine the two parties' duopoly by allowing voters to list both first and second choices on ballots, thus registering their true preferences without risk of electing their least-favored candidate.

Election 2000 offered ample proof of how far the United States has fallen from Lincoln's grand vision of a government of the people, by the people, and for the people. But the founders were careful to build into our system a wondrous capacity for self-correction: we Americans can, after all, vote the scoundrels out, reform whatever laws we don't like, and cast the money-changers out of the temple of democracy. If an aroused populace seizes on this potential, there is no telling what miracles might occur.

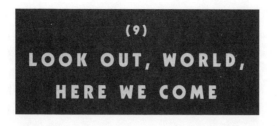

(9)

LOOK OUT, WORLD, HERE WE COME

When Beldrich Moldan told me, "As a European, you may like the United States or not like the United States, but you know it's the future," he was more right than he knew. A former environment minister of the Czech Republic, Moldan made that statement during an interview in 1994. In 2001 I returned to his hometown of Prague to find a McDonald's occupying one corner of Wenceslas Square, steps away from the old Parliament building. Down the block was a Starbucks. Also fronting on the square were dozens of other shiny retail shops. Automatic teller machines dotted the Old Town, and I had brunch one day in an Internet café whose English-language menu and self-consciously funky ambience would have fit perfectly in Seattle or San Francisco.

I sometimes wished Moldan could have joined me during the rest of my trip for this book; he would have seen that the world's Americanization is even more pronounced when one ventures beyond Europe. One manifestation of America's global reach is the ubiquity of English as the language of international business, tourism, and communication. Others are the proliferation of fast food, the rise of junk TV, and the increasing adoption of American consumption habits in general, all of which feed individualism, accelerate the pace of daily life, and encourage in foreigners the very tendencies they criticize as boorish in Americans. Undergirding all this is a less visible form of influence. More and more nations have adopted the pro-corporate, free market ideology that has dominated policymaking in the United States for the past quarter century. What the media call globalization therefore ends up being Americanization by and large, even when conducted by corporations with no particular connection to the United States.

My first stop with Moldan would be Mpande, a small village in South Africa, where I would introduce him to Basiswe and Basiswa, fifteen-year-old twins I met one morning while walking the dusty path to the neighboring village. The twins, tall, lean girls, were headed the other way but happy to stop and give me directions (when they weren't giggling at the novelty of speaking with a white traveler). Most local kids knew no English; the school was too far away and expensive for them. But these girls were fluent, thanks in part to lessons from their older brother, a teacher in Port Elizabeth, an industrial city hundreds of kilometers away.

The instant they learned I was from America, the twins looked at each other and joyfully shrieked, "R. Kelly!" It turned out they had seen the young American singer on television, and they yearned for him as only teenage girls can yearn. The louder twin, Basiswa, announced, "I will marry R. Kelly." She asked if I knew him. After all, she knew everyone who lived in her village, and R. Kelly and I both lived in America.

When I mentioned that one of my brothers was an actor,

Basiswa asked, "Like Jackie Chan?" Once again, my reply disappointed (my brother does stage work, not karate crime movies). Basiswa loved Jackie Chan's movies. When she grew up, she said, "I want to be a movie producer and make movies like Jackie Chan's movies. Then I will be rich." Her sister giggled. "And then you will marry R. Kelly?"

What made this exchange remarkable was that these girls were not city kids. Go to Cape Town or Johannesburg and you can find most of the creature comforts available in any European or American city—satellite television, record shops, movie theaters—so it's not surprising that South Africa's urban youth are conversant with American pop culture. (Remember Malcolm Adams, from the start of this book?) But Basiswa and Basiswe lived in a remote, humble village where most inhabitants had no electricity, much less television. Nevertheless, they were MTV fans.

Mpande is located at the southernmost edge of the Transkei, the historically undeveloped region of South Africa where Nelson Mandela was born. Like so much of the country, the Transkei is a land of jaw-dropping natural beauty: craggy mountains, enormous vistas, rolling hills dotted with cattle, sparkling rivers cutting through steep green valleys. To reach Mpande, you exit the modern highway at Umtata, the regional capital, and drive south for the last hundred kilometers. The farther you go, the worse the road gets, until finally it is a rutted track on which the truck bounces and heaves like a bucking horse. The village itself, a scattering of conical grass huts, is perched on a series of hills overlooking a magnificent stretch of Indian Ocean coastline.

The day after I got there, I found myself enjoying the hospitality of a family reunion. A group of young men, laughing and weaving with drink, were leaving an outdoor gathering down the road when one of them addressed me in poor English and insisted I join the party. The succulent aroma of a cow roasting over an open fire wafted toward me, and soon other partygoers were welcoming me with smiles and greetings in the Xhosa language.

I was ushered into a squarish building that had no windows, only a door flap, so inside was more shadow than light. On the left were three rows of women, seated on the floor, legs stretched straight in front of them, wearing head scarves of yellow, scarlet, and sky blue. To the right were the men, seated on low stools and overturned plastic buckets. In between was a narrow aisle where one or another person got up to sing or dance. A woman in the front drummed a stick against a plastic tub and led everyone in song. Metal pails of warm mealie beer (extracted from corn) were passed around, everyone drinking from the same container. The mood was festive and jovial until one man stood, waited for quiet, and delivered a short, somber speech. The group listened with respectfully tilted heads and murmured assent and then sang a sort of hymn that was very beautiful. The man next to me, who spoke very little English, said that the speech and song were for a deceased family elder.

It was late afternoon now. The only light in the hut came from whatever rays of sun beamed through the door, so it was quite dim. Later, a fire would be built for light and warmth, but wood was too precious to waste, so for now everyone simply sat in the ever-darkening softness, singing, clapping, and passing the beer. It was nice to be reminded that electricity is not essential to human happiness; in fact, except for the last hundred years or so, humans have lived without it. And while modern humans have certainly gained a great deal from electricity, we have lost something as well—the rooted earthly connection that comes with waking and sleeping by the rhythms of the sun and staring at firelight rather than TV screens.

Mpande was fascinating because modernity's invasion of traditional society was so visible there. Teenagers like Basiswe and Basiswa—who thrilled to the high-tech love songs of flavor-of-the-month pop stars a world away—lived in the same village as grown-ups who still made music with their own hands and mouths while drinking homemade beer in an unlit grass hut.

Critics of globalization (as it is currently practiced) deplore its destruction of traditional cultures, the way its promotion of materialist individualism crowds out values of community and sustainability. There is no question this occurs, but the totality of the issue is more complex. From my travels it seems clear that many people in traditional cultures welcome the invasion of modernity, and for comprehensible reasons. I had spent months in rural Africa (in Kenya, Uganda, and Sudan) before this trip, but until Mpande I had never witnessed one common housekeeping chore: the application of fresh cow dung to the floor of a hut. Just as Americans might polish their wooden floors every couple of weeks, so rural African housekeepers (invariably women) resurface their floors of dried dung to reduce dust. The woman I observed got on her hands and knees with a pail of fresh dung and a basin of water (fetched from the distant river, of course). She mixed water and dung in her hands until it had the consistency of a thick soup, then wiped this substance across the floor with her palm, making long, smooth arcs. The smell was as you'd expect, but to her it was as routine as loading the dishwasher is for an American. Routine but not, I think, pleasant. Who could blame this woman for wanting more modernity in her life?

The rub is that members of traditional societies tend not to appreciate that along with modern technology and convenience comes unanticipated baggage; before they know it, customs and values they hold dear are vanishing into the air. The process is not new; the Nigerian writer Chinua Achebe brilliantly dissected the transforming effects of modernization on rural Africa in his 1958 novel *Things Fall Apart*. But the speed and scope of modernity's global advance over the past ten years are unprecedented; as Mpande shows, it has now penetrated the most impoverished corners of the world's most impoverished continent. And for better and worse, nothing defines modernity more than America.

THE AMERICANIZATION OF JAPAN

My next stop with Moldan would be at the opposite end of the rich-poor divide, in Japan. Of the thirty nations I have visited, none copies the United States more enthusiastically than Japan does. "We always imitate America," Haruko, an art historian and mother in her mid-forties, told me with a nervous laugh in the ancient town of Nara. "Maybe it's envy, mixed with admiration. Japanese people love to rank things, and the United States is ranked by everyone as number one. So Japanese think, 'If we can be number two, that's pretty good!' "

I was surprised by how much Japan reminded me of the United States. In a land with one of the most delicate cuisines on earth, fast food was everywhere. (I later learned that the top two restaurants in sales volume were McDonald's and Kentucky Fried Chicken.) There was the same suburban sprawl as in the United States (or worse), the same overpackaging of consumer items (each piece of fruit individually

wrapped), the same throwaway mentality (carryout food en-
cased in plastic, chopsticks discarded after one use). The
meditative simplicity advocated by Buddhism jarred with the
explosion of American-style twenty-four-hour convenience
stores, just as Japan's environmental reputation was undercut
by its fascination with advertising, glorification of consumption, and worship of automobiles.

Japan's emulation of the United States could be amusing at
times, especially when it involved the English language. Japanese study English in school for six years, but because conversation is rarely practiced, most end up unable to speak it.
One night in Kyoto, I was checking out the main drag and
happened into a gigantic amusement center: seven stories of
cacophonous noise, computer games, and pop culture. Hollywood icons were plentifully represented. There was even
bowling, the epitome of retro-hip back in the United States.
The management was doing its best to make bowling look
cool, plastering the walls with such cheerful quasi-English ex-
hortations as "You can do it! Do you like bowling? Let's play
bowling. Breaking down the pins and get hot communication."

Japan's fascination with all things American seemed odd in
some respects, for in fundamental ways the two cultures could
hardly be more different. America embodies ambitious individualism par excellence. In Japan, as the saying goes, "The
nail that sticks out gets pounded down," and the group takes
precedence. Of course, opposites can attract; the personal
freedom Americans take for granted is no doubt appealing in
a culture of uniformity, and the creativity born of such freedom may account for Japan's love of American pop culture.

But what about history? The United States did drop two
atom bombs on Japan; did they leave no residue of resentment? Not much, it seems. Younger people I questioned saw

the bombs as ancient events, irrelevant to today. Older people were less dismissive but never angry. "People were excited when the war ended. We were hungry and tired," a retired literature professor named Takama told me while we shared a lookout bench on Mount Hiei, the sacred mountain of Japanese Buddhism. What's more, explained Masao Kase, a publishing and clothing executive in Tokyo, "most Japanese at that time did not know what happened in Hiroshima and Nagasaki. There was total censorship. Later, during the six-year American occupation of Japan, General MacArthur skillfully used propaganda to deflect any anger that Japanese people had about the war onto the Japanese army, which was blamed for starting the war."

The truth, added Kase, is that "Japanese love all things foreign, but America is the most imitated because it is the most visible and the easiest to copy. French food, Italian art—these are much harder to copy than American television, fashion, or shopping styles." Indeed, Japan's rise to become an economic superpower after World War II was based on imitating American production models: building electronic goods just as well as America did but, thanks to cheaper labor, selling them at lower prices on the world market.

Nowadays, the Americanization of Japan takes many more forms, including the gradual abandonment among the young of the practice of removing one's shoes before entering the house. "My own house is an example," said Haruko, the art historian. "It has only one traditional Japanese room, with tatami mats on the floor. All the other rooms have Western-style chairs and sofas. I can sit in the traditional Japanese way [legs folded back, feet tucked under the buttocks] for only one hour at a time before the pain is too much. My mother can sit like that forever."

What Haruko, like most Japanese I met, liked best about America were the creations of Hollywood. She could speak at eloquent length about the art and temples of ancient Japan, but she was absolutely possessed by Hollywood movies. The *Superman* series was one favorite, and *Star Wars* seemed to hold an almost religious significance for her. She had seen the movies countless times, bought the memorabilia, monitored the web sites, debated other fans about plot lines. She seemed genuinely agitated about what might happen in Episode II, *Attack of the Clones*, and anxiously asked me whether it had been released yet in the United States. "I am very eager for this movie to come to Japan," she said. "I must see—how can that nice blond boy turn into Darth Vader?"

THE NBA COMES TO CHINA AND SICILY

The modern American empire colonizes minds, not territory. It does so primarily through its dominance of perhaps the most important technology of the last fifty years: the screen, in all of its varied applications. Once upon a time, the outside world learned about the United States mainly on movie screens—Hollywood's version of life in America. Later, movies were supplemented by television and then video, which reach more (and more remote) places and operate twenty-four hours a day. The same two advantages adhere to the Internet, which now links computer screens around the world. All these technologies are aimed above all at youth. All reflect and extend the global dominance of English. All can carry different, even contradictory, impulses but are united by an overriding commitment to commerce. Soon, all will be lashed together into a single electronic box of communication, consumerism, and potential control.

Americans are the best marketers in the world and the screen is our most powerful tool. Via the screen, we convince others to want what we specialize in producing: a consumerist definition of happiness. MTV, probably the single vehicle most responsible for homogenizing tastes and boosting consumption among youth around the world, was an American invention. Launched in 1980, by 1998 it claimed to reach 273.5 million households in eighty-three different countries (though such numbers were often hype—more marketing). The network's success was a function of sheer demography. Infant mortality rates fell in the Third World in the 1960s and 1970s while birthrates climbed. The result was a boom of young people; today, one billion of the world's six billion people are teenagers. A 1996 marketing survey of teens in forty-five countries, conducted for Coca-Cola, Burger King, and other corporations and quoted in Naomi Klein's *No Logo*, found that 85 percent of middle-class teenagers watched MTV every day. The rise of the so-called New World Teen, said a New York advertising executive involved with the survey, is "one of the greatest marketing opportunities of all time."

"There isn't a lot of angst, it's just unbridled consumerism," MTV's chief executive officer, Tom Freston, said when describing the content of MTV India. That consumerism ranges far beyond music to include fashion, sport, snacks, soft drinks—all the accoutrements of a hip American lifestyle. Traveling the world in the early 1990s, I often saw images of Michael Jackson and Madonna pasted on walls of buses and schools in the Third World. By 1997 Michael Jordan had taken over. One of my environmental sources in Beijing, a university professor with a sixteen-year-old daughter, said that his daughter and her friends had become as infatuated with Jordan "as with a movie star" and now wanted Chicago Bulls jackets for their birthdays. In 2001, in Agrigento, Sicily, a young man from Madagascar gave me a discerning critique of the Los Angeles Lakers' performance in the second game of the National Basketball Association championship the night before.

How did the NBA become cool to global youth? American domination of foreign media markets has grown astronomically over the past thirty years, with the sharpest growth occurring in the 1990s. By the end of the 1990s, writes Robert W. McChesney in *Rich Media, Poor Democracy*, the film, music, and TV industries were relying on sales outside the United States for between 50 and 70 percent of their revenues. Benjamin Barber reports in *Jihad vs. McWorld* that by 1998 American movies dominated top-ten box office listings across the European continent, accounting for 60 percent of revenues in France and 95 percent in the United Kingdom. Sales of American music and TV shows were similarly robust, not only in Europe but in the so-called emerging markets of Asia, Africa, and South America.

Defenders of the American entertainment industry argue that they simply have a superior product; foreigners vote with their wallets and prefer what Hollywood offers. But do audiences get what they like, or like what they get? It is a given country's media industry, not its citizens, that decides which movies, TV shows, and musical acts are offered for purchase. And nowadays, media industries in Europe and elsewhere are dominated by the same handful of transnational corporations that dominate the American market: Disney, AOL Time Warner, Viacom, Sony, News Corporation, Bertelsmann,

AT&T. Although these corporations naturally compete with one another at times, they also collaborate to create a business climate in which all can profit. One such occasion arose in 1997, when the European Union attempted to limit the American takeover of European mass culture. The EU proposed a law requiring that at least 50 percent of the television programs shown in Europe be produced in Europe; it was defeated by fierce lobbying by Europe's own media corporations, which wanted to buy more programs from their American brethren, not fewer.

"What the Americans have industrialized as 'entertainment' we in Europe call 'culture.'" So said Luciana Castellina, a European parliamentarian who addressed a conference on "European Society and the American Way" that I attended in Italy in May 2001. (The conference setting alone bespoke the gulf between American and European sensibilities; it was held in a stone convent in Tuscany that had been founded in 980 A.D. Occupying the entire wall behind Castellina was a stunningly well-preserved fresco of the Last Supper, dating from the 1400s.) What disturbed Castellina was not only America's commercialism but its crowding out of Europe's homegrown culture. "We Europeans are now more familiar with the images and faces of the United States than of Europe," she complained. "We recognize New York City and Los Angeles but not Berlin or Madrid."

REAGAN AND THE TRIUMPH
OF WEALTH, PART TWO

The Americanization of global culture is a complex story featuring many players, but one of its stars is Ronald Reagan, himself a former Hollywood screen actor. Reagan's deregulation of broadcasting in the United States sent ripples across the world. By allowing corporations to own not just seven but twelve television, twelve FM, and twelve AM radio stations, Reagan gave media corporations countless billions of dollars in new revenue. This financial infusion helped the corporations to expand their presence in overseas markets, but even more decisive over time was the power of the American example. The gigantic sums of money that deregulated television began to make for American companies spurred their foreign counterparts to redouble efforts to gain similar opportunities in their home countries, where broadcasting was usually dominated by public entities such as the BBC. The story is complex and varies by country, but in general such efforts succeeded; commercial television experienced enormous growth around the world in the 1990s.

The result has been a proliferation of the junkiest of junk television. By the late 1990s, an average of one billion people a day were watching *Baywatch*, the moronic Hollywood drama starring lifeguards in scanty swimsuits. In Egypt, one-third of the programs shown on the state-run television networks are crime shows from the United States, with the result that Steven Seagal and Chuck Norris are household names among children. Across Europe, the triumph of commercial priorities is so pervasive that even public broadcasting stalwarts like the BBC and its Dutch and Swedish counterparts have launched commercial divisions and begun to broadcast advertising. Wherever one turns, the offerings on television screens are looking more and more like those of the United States. Americans' television-viewing habits appear to be spreading as well. French children aged four to eleven averaged nearly two hours of television a day in 1997, a 10 percent increase from the year before.

The media sector reveals, in microcosm, Reagan's greater

achievement: by transforming America's economy, he changed how capitalism operated throughout the world. With help from his ideological soul mate, British prime minister Margaret Thatcher, Reagan challenged the prevailing assumptions within the major capitalist countries about the proper extent of the welfare state and the regulation of capital. Get government off of business's back and out of charity work, he argued, and everyone will be better off. In Britain as in the United States, this approach yielded a burst of economic growth, a widening of the gap between rich and poor, and an erosion of transportation, health, and other public services. Crucially, and perhaps unwittingly on Reagan's part, it also pressured other countries to adopt similar free market policies, if only to remain competitive in the world market.

How so? By cutting taxes and regulations, Reagan effectively lowered the operating costs of American corporations. This naturally aided their expansion into foreign markets, but it also gave ammunition to Reagan's ideological allies abroad. Corporate and right-wing forces in other countries could now justify the idea of scaling back their own welfare states, cutting taxes, and deregulating corporations by citing the need to remain competitive with the Americans. Meanwhile, Reagan was also pushing deregulation of international commerce—the so-called free trade agenda of opening foreign nations to corporate investment and removing the kinds of barriers that the European Union later tried to erect against American television programming. America's overwhelming influence within the World Trade Organization, the International Monetary Fund, and the World Bank helped ensure that this free market vision carried the day, especially in weaker economies in Asia, Africa, and Latin America. Just as globalization has been largely Americanization, so Reagan's version of free market capitalism has become the global norm.

Nowhere have these trends combined more ostentatiously than in Italy, where tycoon Silvio Berlusconi has made a crusade of copying Reaganism. Berlusconi, who began as a real estate magnate from Milan, had by the early 1990s accumulated a formidable media empire, including three private television networks as well as Italy's largest publisher of newspapers, magazines, and books. He then set out to acquire direct political power, seizing the opening provided by the corruption scandals that discredited Italy's governing parties to offer himself as a reform candidate in the 1994 elections. Ample, adoring coverage from his own media outlets gave his candidacy instant credibility. He ended up as prime minister in a coalition with the neofascist National Alliance and the separatist Lombardy League, but it collapsed after seven months. He ran again in 2001, to the dismay of some in Europe. *The Economist* declared him unfit to govern, noting that as prime minister he would control not only Italy's three largest private TV networks but also its three publicly owned networks. Nevertheless, the week I arrived in Italy to begin my travels for this book, he was elected, decisively.

"Of course, Berlusconi's control of television helped him win this election, but not in the direct propaganda sense of his companies saying, 'Vote for me,'" said Paula Biagini, a high school teacher from Florence who was seated next to me at the "European Society and the American Way" conference. "He was helped more by the indirect effect of his television shows, which glorify the American lifestyle and economic model and discourage critical thinking. Many of our youth voted for Berlusconi. I know from my students that they believe in the American model they see on TV. Fewer young people are going on to universities—we have a serious short-age of engineers now—because they are instead going to work in the shoe and eyeglass factories up north to make money. They don't worry about the future. They think they will be able to jump from one job to another and buy a new car every six months, just like in America."

Youth are not the only targets of America's colonizing of minds, nor is the screen the only means of transmission. But whatever the age bracket and however the message is con-veyed, the result is to spread a monoculture of tastes, values, and behavior. More and more people around the world now wear the same brands of clothing, consume the same food and drink, watch the same movies, listen to the same music, and in doing so they take their cues largely from American corpo-rate marketeers. In Sweden, for example, if you drive west from Stockholm to the Norwegian border, you now find a newly constructed McDonald's every forty kilometers. Jan Leuwenhagen, an editor at Sweden's leading newspaper, *Da-gens Nyheter*, recalls that drinking Coke got a person criticized in the 1970s for helping to promote American influence in Sweden, but no longer. "I have three kids," he told me. "I don't remember exactly when it was, but at a certain point we started to buy Coke for Saturday nights as a special treat. Now, if the kids hadn't moved out, Coke would be competing with milk even on workdays."

The day I left Agrigento, *La Repubblica* carried a quote from the Italian writer Umberto Eco: "Today when a traveler returns home, he has nothing to tell his friends. Because everywhere he goes, people dress the same and act the same as they do at home." They talk the same, too. Young people everywhere are learning English and dropping tongues that have less currency in the globalized world. Echoing a comment I heard numerous times in Sicily, a restaurant manager in Agrigento told me that he rarely spoke Sicilian anymore; even with his parents he spoke Italian. "I don't quite know why," he said. "It just seems more sophisticated, more modern." He agreed this would mean the death of the dialect, which he called "a shame," but he saw no change ahead. Kids were taught English but not Sicilian in school, and they learned still more English while playing with their computers. "When we were kids," he recalled, "soccer was our life. We'd play for hours and hours and come home all sweaty. Now kids surf computers."

Even critics of the American way find themselves captivated by it. Hany, the engineer in Cairo who criticized Americans for having too many toothpaste brands, admitted that Egyptians, too, are now finding less time for loved ones. "You invented globalization, your culture is all over the world, and here is no exception," he said as, without irony, he lit another Marlboro. "Grown children have less to do with their parents now, you see half as many attendees at funerals—people are busy with their own lives, making money. We care less about each other and more about our salaries, mobile phones, and TV sets. I can't say I like it, but we are becoming more like you."

DOES THE WORLD NEED MORE MCDONALD'S?

So there is a lot of evidence that Beldrich Moldan was right about America being the future. Globalization is one of the defining trends of today's world, and it has been American corporations, policies, and values that have driven the process. But there is nothing inevitable about the continuation of

Americanized globalization, especially since the September 11 attacks have shaken the faith of some of its most prominent supporters.

Resistance is rising not only from the protesters whose demonstrations in Seattle, Prague, Porto Alegre, and elsewhere have thrown World Bank and IMF bureaucrats on the defensive. Opposition is also coming from mainstream civil society and being expressed in conventional political processes. I write these words in a week when Italy experienced its first general strike in twenty years; millions of unionists and supporters took to the streets to oppose the Berlusconi government's attempt to deregulate the nation's labor market in the name of global competitiveness. And Britain's Labour government has just announced plans to restore health, transportation, and other public services ravaged by more than twenty years of budget cuts, and to do so by taking the politically risky step of raising taxes.

The issue is not globalization or no globalization, for technological and other trends make continued global integration inevitable; rather, the issue is what kind of globalization will be pursued. "The media is always trying to tag us with this anti-globalization label," Susan George, a founder of the French-based group ATTAC (Association for the Taxation of Financial Transactions for the Aid of Citizens), told me in Paris. "But we reject that. We aren't anti-globalization, we are pro–social justice and human solidarity. We insist that another world is possible."

The core of the critics' critique is that the current form of globalization has punished the world's poor and working-class majority while fabulously rewarding the rich and corporate elite. Furthermore, because the free market model values economic growth above other considerations, it tends to damage the environment, defund public services, and threaten labor and human rights.

Critics accuse the corporations that propel globalization of causing a "race to the bottom"—shifting production to countries that wink at sweatshops and toxic emissions while forcing workers in wealthier nations to choose between lower wages and unemployment. So-called free trade, they add, is anything but. The World Trade Organization, argues economist Martin Khor, "is about free trade *and* protectionism at the same time. It's about a double standard that continues to protect rich countries against products that poor countries are good at exporting." Rich-country trade barriers cost poor countries $100 billion a year in forgone export revenues, according to the World Bank.

The critics blame the structural adjustment programs imposed by the IMF for, among other things, the impoverishment of the Russian middle class in the 1990s (as the nation underwent a "shock treatment" transition to free markets that threw millions out of work) and the widespread destitution that followed the financial meltdown in Asia in 1997. In Indonesia, for example, the IMF ordered bank closures in a nation with no deposit insurance, provoking riots; unemployment soared to 20 percent and 100 million people, half the country, were soon living on less than a dollar a day.

In short, critics argue, the American free market model has yielded the same results overseas that it has in the United States: stupendous wealth for a small elite, stagnation or worse for almost everyone else. The World Bank itself has admitted that "globalization appears to increase poverty and inequality." The United Nations Human Development Report of 1999 reported that "the income gap between the fifth of the world's people living in the richest countries and the fifth in the poorest doubled from 1960 to 1990, from 30 to 1 to 60 to 1. By 1998 it had jumped again, with the gap widening to an astonishing 78 to 1." Meanwhile, giant corporations control more and more of the world economy. The Institute for Policy Studies, a left-of-center research group in Washington, D.C., reported in its 2000 study, "Top 200," that "of the largest 100 economies in the world, 52 are now corporations; only 48 are countries." Such corporate control makes increased inequality all but certain, for it is by buying up competitors and shedding workers that the corporations grow. While the two hundred largest corporations account for 30 percent of global economic activity, they employ less than 1 percent of the global workforce.

It took the tragedy of September 11 before proponents began to admit that globalization was perhaps not the panacea they had promised. Suddenly there was an appreciation that poverty, while not directly responsible for terrorism, could at least nourish the despair and frustration that can give rise to violence. Kofi Annan, the secretary-general of the United Nations, warned business and political elites at the World Economic Forum in New York in February 2002 that "the perception among many is that [extreme poverty and inequality are] the fault of globalization, and that globalization is driven by a global elite . . . represented by the people who attend this gathering." Bill Gates declared, "We need a discussion about whether the rich world is giving back what it should in the developing world." A month later, the *New York Times*, itself a frequent champion of globalization, reported on a conference of world leaders in Monterrey, Mexico, to discuss fighting poverty. The leaders now recognized that, in the *Times*'s words, "the vast majority of people living in Africa, Latin America, Central Asia and the Middle East are no better off today than they were in 1989, when the fall of the Berlin Wall allowed capitalism to spread worldwide at a rapid rate."

These were stunning reversals of opinion, but what changes they may bring to the American model of globalization remain to be seen. One proposal that has attracted support not only from critics like ATTAC but world leaders like British prime minister Tony Blair is to launch a global Marshall Plan, modeled on the effort the United States mounted after World War II to revive the battered economies of Europe through aid, investment, debt relief, and preferential trade and technology arrangements. African heads of state had proposed a similar idea prior to the September 11 attacks. That program called for African nations to get their own houses in order—halting wars and corruption, upholding human rights, ensuring transparency in government decisions—in return for a major increase in assistance from rich countries aimed at basic development needs: health care, education, jobs. What remains is to put these ideas into practice.

The globalization debate will shape the world economy— and therefore the fight against poverty, disease, environmental degradation, and terrorism—for years to come. Needless to say, the American role will be critical. As with international environmental policy, the United States wields what amounts to veto power over globalization policy. It will be difficult to launch a meaningful Marshall Plan and reverse the current "race to the bottom" if the United States insists on going its own way. Americans therefore need to reflect on what kind of globalization we wish to stand for. Does the planet really need more McDonald's? Or is another world possible?

(10)
AMERICA THE BEAUTIFUL

There are two memories I will always carry with me from the journey for this book. Each involves a volcano, and each, I think, says something important about America.

In the year 79 A.D., the Roman empire was the mightiest power on earth. Its armies were undefeated, its technology unsurpassed, its wealth beyond measure. Among its many holdings was the city of Pompeii, a port on Italy's west coast, a few miles from present-day Naples. Pompeii's strategic location gave it great military and trade advantages, and its ten thousand inhabitants enjoyed a high standard of living. The city's forum was modeled on Rome's, with a magnificent basilica, temples fronted by tall Ionic columns, beautifully carved marble statues, and splendid views of Mount Vesuvius, which towered over the northern skyline. Homes in the wealthier part of town featured running water, shaded gardens, and fountains lined by mosaics in a rainbow of colors. Pompeii's main street was the Via dell'Abbondanza—Abundance Street.

And then one day there was fire on the mountain. First came the sound—a terrifying roar as powerful explosions shook the earth. Then came the river of flame. Volcanic rock, burning so hot it had liquefied, burst from the bowels of Vesuvius and gushed toward the city below, covering everything in its path. The avalanche reached Pompeii so quickly that townspeople had no time to run. By the time the volcano had spent itself, the city had disappeared, buried beneath twenty feet of lava and ash.

Because the lava covered everything so thoroughly, Pompeii is today one of the best-preserved cities of antiquity. When I toured the site, I found walking among its ruins an unnerving yet exciting experience, a visit backward in time to a past that had been captured at the exact moment of death. Everything looked so lifelike, I could almost see the ghosts of those who perished that day. (Indeed, plaster casts showed the death poses of some victims, many of whom appear to have been sleeping.) Most striking were the artifacts of daily life, such as the thermopolium, a café whose specialty of serving hot drinks was plain from the bowl-shaped indentations in a countertop facing the Via dell'Abbondanza. Down the street was a laundry, around the corner a bordello with bawdy frescoes on the wall, across town a stadium and parade ground for Roman imperial troops. How similar the human habits of then and now! And all extinguished in an instant.

Three months after my visit to Pompeii, the American empire was assaulted by its own river of fire in the city of New York. This time, death and destruction arrived on the wings of hate, not the whims of nature. Victims were buried alive beneath ash and rubble not by geological chance but human intent—by a carefully plotted, perfectly executed strike intended to show that, as mastermind Osama bin Laden put it, "America is much weaker than it appears." Thousands perished, millions were terrified. Once again, the vulnerability of even the richest and most powerful civilization stood revealed, and survivors were engulfed by grief, fear, and bewilderment.

Barely one year later, it is still too soon to understand the full significance of the September 11 attacks; how important they will look twenty, much less two thousand, years from now is impossible to know. Were they an isolated event, or the first blow in a protracted war? Will they lead to a reshuffling of global power relations, or reinforce American preeminence? Will they spur cooperation against poverty, disease, tyranny, and other social blights that, whatever their causative links to terrorism, are abominations in their own right? Or will they be invoked to justify intensified militarism and security restrictions? Much will depend on what lessons are drawn from the tragedy, by Americans and foreigners alike.

It quickly became a truism that September 11 had changed everything; the world was said to be a different place now. The more time that passes, however, the less true that seems to be. It's the same world as before, though it's not clear that we understand it any better.

Attitudes of average Americans have not changed much since the September 11 attacks, pollsters have reported. Americans are paying more attention to foreign news now—a positive development—but our views about what is going on, both at home and abroad, seem little changed. Extensive surveys released in May 2002 at the annual meeting of the American Association for Public Opinion Research indicate that Americans' opinions about religion, government, civil liberties, and other such issues have remained quite stable since September 11. President Bush's high job approval ratings, for example, reflected support for the presidency in a time of national crisis, rather than a surge in support for Bush's specific actions.

Foreigners' views of America have reverted to form as well. "We are all Americans now," many of them declared after September 11. But such solidarity quickly faded as Washington revealed itself to be the same old empire everyone knew and didn't much love: impregnable in its self-regard, untroubled by double standards, ever-ready to shoot its guns but never to listen. Though foreigners were initially reassured when the Bush administration went to the trouble of assembling a coalition to attack Afghanistan, this was wishful thinking; Washington left no doubt that it would proceed alone if necessary. Bush called his war against terrorism a crusade, a word he soon abandoned for fear of stoking Muslim resentment of Christian domination in medieval times. As months passed, however, and Secretary of Defense Donald Rumsfeld said that "if we have to go into ten or fifteen other countries [to eliminate terrorism], we should do it," "crusade" seemed exactly the right description of the American response. Bush clinched the point with his notorious "axis of evil" speech in January 2002, in which he indicated that the United States was prepared to unilaterally expand the war against terrorism to include Iraq, Iran, and North Korea.

"It was striking how short the period of widespread solidarity and sympathy with the United States was in the wake of September 11," wrote a leading Belgian newspaper, *De Standaard*, a few days later. More alarm bells rang in March after the disclosure of Pentagon plans that envisioned offensive use of nuclear weapons against those three countries as well as Libya and Syria—a stunning repudiation of the long-standing global consensus that nuclear weapons were for deterrence only. America's swaggering unilateralism provoked rebuke even from such traditional cheerleaders as Anatole Kaletsky, usually an exuberantly pro-American columnist for the *Times* of London. "The greatest danger to America's dominant position today is not Islamic fundamentalism," Kaletsky wrote. "It is the arrogance of American power."

But Washington was only getting started. In April the Bush administration forced the removal of the scientist heading the Intergovernmental Panel on Climate Change (he had displeased Exxon Mobil), as well as the head of the Organization for the Prohibition of Chemical Weapons (he was an obstacle to American designs on Iraq). It shunned ratifying the International Criminal Court; in an unprecedented step, it even revoked President Clinton's signature on the treaty. Most dramatically, the administration ignored repeated international appeals that it get involved and deter the horrifying escalation of violence in the Middle East; instead, it insisted on pressing its universally unpopular plan to attack Iraq. When the rising death toll finally forced a focus on the West Bank, Washington again stood alone, supporting Israel's invasion of Palestinian cities following repeated suicide bombings. Both official and popular opinion in virtually every country in the world held that Israel was going too far, but Bush seemed more concerned by criticism from right-wing Republicans that he wasn't backing Israel enough.

On the six-month anniversary of September 11, the president pledged to lead humanity to "a peaceful world beyond terror" where "disputes can be settled within the bounds of reason and goodwill and mutual security." But Bush's advisers had separately made it plain that they desired continued American domination of the rest of the world. National security adviser Condoleezza Rice likened today's situation to that immediately following World War II. Just as fifty years ago the threat of Communism led other nations to band together beneath American leadership in the Cold War, Rice argued, so today the threat of terrorism justifies a new phase of American leadership. The Bush administration apparently hoped that the war on terrorism would become, like the Cold War before it, the organizing principle of United States foreign policy. One Cold War, it seems, was not enough, and it's probably no coincidence that Bush officials say the war against terrorism will last another forty to fifty years.

The implications are profound for Americans and non-Americans alike. At home, Bush's war on terrorism has already been advanced as justification for an unprecedented assault on the civil liberties that are America's greatest strength. Meanwhile, urgent domestic needs—health care for the nation's rapidly aging population, job training for its underclass, investments in renewable energy—are being sacrificed on the altar of the corporate welfare system known as the defense budget. The first Cold War made permanent the "military-industrial complex" that President Dwight Eisenhower warned against in his 1960 farewell address. Forty-two years later, the Pentagon budget has little rational relationship to the nation's military needs. Pressure from the weapons makers, the military services, and members of Congress eager to deliver jobs for constituents causes spending to stay high no matter what actual threats face the United States. (The peace dividend promised at the end of the Cold War somehow never did arrive.) This both impoverishes America and directly threatens the rest of the world. What good is a big military if it stays home?

The American public has been wary of overseas military involvement since the Vietnam era, but Bush officials have told reporters on a not-for-attribution basis that September 11 changed all that; now that the United States has been attacked directly, Americans supposedly will be willing to accept combat deaths. Thus the probability of overseas military interventions in the years ahead is high. And since such interventions will likely leave survivors angry at the United States, the chances of retaliatory terrorism will grow. Washington will cite such retaliations as justification for additional interventions, and the cycle will continue. It's the blowback syndrome squared.

As this book went to press, the Bush administration made aggressive militarism into an official doctrine. Speaking in June 2002 at the graduation ceremony for the cadets of the United States Military Academy, President Bush announced that henceforth America would attack presumed enemies preemptively, before they attacked the United States. No longer would Washington sleep while others prepared September 11– or Pearl Harbor–style sneak attacks. America would go on the offensive, striking when and where it saw fit, regardless of such niceties as international law or diplomatic negotiations. Iraq seemed the preferred first target, but the new doctrine left room for strikes against all manner of powers, both states and nonstates. Talk about shooting first and asking questions later! Could the Bush high command have devised a doctrine more likely to alienate allies, infuriate enemies real and imagined, and destabilize international relations? Yet the Bush doctrine provoked no criticism within the nation's political elite; apparently neither the press nor the Democrats saw anything wrong with Wasington appointing itself the world's judge, jury, and executioner.

WELCOME TO THE TWENTY-FIRST CENTURY

After the Vesuvius volcano buried Pompeii, the ancients blamed themselves; clearly, such a tragedy meant that they had angered the gods terribly. America has taken the opposite tack: We are blameless, the September 11 attacks were evil, and God stands with us in our response. One sign of our reaction was how quickly "God Bless America" became the national soundtrack after September 11. Even counterculture figures like Willie Nelson were singing it, and no World Series game was complete without it. After President Bush appeared on-screen during game one to assure the millions watching this most American ritual that "we will defeat the evil ones," the stadium crowd stood, waved American flags, and sang along as Vanessa Williams delivered the harmonious plea that the Almighty "stand beside us, and guide us, through the night with a light from above." A sign in the crowd read "America Fears No One. Play Ball."

Its religious faith and patriotic fervor doubtless helped the United States to weather the difficult period after September 11; the attacks inadvertently served to renew what had been a shriveled sense of national unity. Many Americans were proud to be hated by such despicable men as bin Laden and his followers. But the self-congratulatory mood also had its drawbacks, for it blinded many Americans to the broader implications of the tragedy.

One would think that the resurfacing of anti-Americanism among our closest allies so soon after September 11 might give America pause, make people think. But no. Most discussion, at least as conducted by the nation's political and media elites, has avoided critical introspection about how the United States relates to the rest of the world. In a letter published in London's *Financial Times* shortly after the attacks, Allan Wendt, a former United States ambassador to Slovenia, urged that, beyond pursuing the murderers, "America needs a bit of soul-searching, a hard look at how others see us and why, if we are to cope effectively and wisely with the excruciating dilemma we face today." He also suggested, "We must avoid self-righteousness, the conviction that we are always right and that our way is the only way." Alas, we have done nothing of the kind. The reigning assumption has been that the United States was wronged, period, and anyone who advises soul-searching is only blaming the victim.

It's a tricky problem, because America *was* wronged and bin Laden *is* evil. He and his henchmen should be punished, and such attacks must be deterred in the future. The question is how to do that. Unfortunately, our current approach seems likely to make matters worse, not better.

America faces a puzzling contradiction: We are by traditional measures the most powerful empire in all of human history, yet humanity has entered an era when no country, no matter how powerful, can adequately defend against the prevailing threats to health and security. We emerged as the last superpower at the very time when superpowers are becoming obsolete.

One of the most revealing, though unremarked, developments of the post–September 11 period took place on October 9, 2001, when President Bush met the head of NATO, Lord Robertson, at the White House. In a routine press statement afterward, Bush noted that for the first time in its fifty-two year history, NATO was coming to the defense of the United States. Bush gave no sign that he understood how monumental a development this was, and media coverage in both the United States and Germany (where I was at the time) also ignored it in favor of stressing the two leaders' agreement over the war in Afghanistan. But clearly the larger story was that the United States, which had founded NATO to defend Europe against Soviet attack during the Cold War, was now the one that needed defending. There are moments in history when one event crystallizes a broader trend, and this seemed to be one of them.

NATO's reversal illustrated what some analysts had been arguing for years: the guiding assumptions of the Cold War are out of date. Military force no longer guarantees supremacy: on September 11 the world's mightiest military was unable to stop a handful of killers armed only with box cutters and a willingness to die for the cause. National sovereignty, though still relevant, is not necessarily decisive in an era of Internet communication, twenty-four-hour financial markets, and global manufacturing systems. The threats of the new era are global and can only be combated globally. Climate change, for example, can wreck economies and crash food production without firing a shot, and only joint action to reduce greenhouse gas emissions will lower the risk. AIDS, malaria, and other diseases that have overrun inadequate public health systems in the Third World ignore national borders, just as immigrants made desperate by poverty and oppression swarm across them. On its own, no country can defend against such threats, not even the United States. Welcome to the twenty-first century.

In the face of these changes, the Bush administration remains committed to a unilateralist, domineering foreign policy that promises to make the global situation worse for Americans and foreigners alike. Rather than attacking poverty and injustice in order to drain the swamps that give rise to terrorism, Bush's preference for muscular diplomacy will encourage more blowback. Rather than protecting the natural ecosystems that make life on earth possible, his refusal to limit greenhouse gas emissions or otherwise inconvenience polluting industries promises to accelerate the decline. Rather than shrinking the unconscionable gap between rich and poor in the interest of both human decency and social stability, Bush's free trade vision of development will increase it.

Kofi Annan has it right when he cautions that poverty alone does not cause terrorism. "The poor have enough burdens without being considered likely terrorists simply because they are poor," the United Nations secretary-general said in a March 2002 speech. But Annan added, "Where massive and systematic political, economic and social inequalities are found, and where no legitimate means of addressing them exists, an environment is created in which peaceful solutions all too often lose out against extreme and violent alternatives." Recognition of this truth helped put the issue of poverty back on the global agenda after September 11, with mainstream business and political leaders suddenly showing new interest in the arguments that development advocates had been making for years.

Bush, however, remained unengaged. His advisers were careful to make him appear concerned, staging a White House photo opportunity with Bono, the rock star and debt-relief advocate, at which Bush proposed increasing the United States foreign aid budget by $10 billion over the next three years. But compare that to his request for military spending and the administration's priorities become clear. Bush urged increasing America's gargantuan military budget by $48 billion a year—an amount larger than the *entire* military budget of any other nation on earth, and twelve times larger on an annual basis than his proposed development aid increase. What's more, Bush made the additional foreign aid conditional on poor nations accepting more of the free trade policies that have slashed their social safety nets, devastated their agricultural sectors, and strengthened multinational corporations' influence over their economies. "To be serious about poverty," Bush declared, "we must be serious about expanding trade."

Bush is a right-winger, so it's natural that he embraces a pro-corporate view of the world. But it's worth noting that conservatives overseas espouse more nuanced and generous approaches to these common problems. French president Jacques Chirac has endorsed an expansive targeted increase in development aid, which he would fund by taxing the corporations that benefit so handsomely from globalization. In Germany, Edmund Stoiber, the conservative challenger to Chancellor Gerhard Schröder, questioned the wisdom of a war to overthrow Saddam Hussein, even as Stoiber urged closer relations between Germany and the United States.

As for terrorism, Bush appears to think it is something committed by "evil" people who can be stopped if only enough guns are fired. Other conservatives recognize that the fight must be a two-pronged effort, combining the stick of police work (targeted surveillance and arrests more than massive air raids and invasions) with the carrot of democracy and development. "The only way to fight terrorism in the long term is to fight the causes of terrorism," Quentin Peel, a writer for the *Financial Times*, has argued. "That means tackling the misery and despair in countries such as Afghanistan. It means striving with every means available to bring peace to the Middle East. . . . Fighting terrorists with the traditional tools of war will not work. It will only bring them more recruits."

The Middle East offers heartbreaking proof. The hardline approach Israel has taken under Prime Minister Ariel Sharon has only fueled Palestinian rage and frustration, thus guaranteeing more reprisals and bloodshed. There is no excuse for terrorism, but there are explanations. When people suffer injustice and oppression, when their lands are occupied, when they are endlessly humiliated, when they are beaten or worse for expressing dissident political opinions, violence can seem their only alternative; and if they face an overwhelmingly better-armed opponent, the violence may be expressed as terrorism against civilians. Suicide bombings are wrong, but they will remain a temptation until underlying injustices are addressed.

The best inoculation against terrorism is real democracy, which should be the United States' strong point and sometimes is. But none of our allies in the Middle East are real democracies (Israel comes closest, but its disenfranchisement of the Palestinians cancels out its parliamentary practices), and our record is pretty spotty elsewhere as well. In the name of fighting terrorism, the Bush administration has greatly increased its backing of the dictators who rule the "stan" nations of Central Asia: Uzbekistan, Kazakhstan, Tajikistan, Turkmenistan, and Kyrgyzstan. As reporter Christian Caryl pointed out in *The New York Review of Books*, "In the most egregious case of all, the U.S. has been lavishing praise and benefits on Uzbekistan's [president Islam] Karimov—notwithstanding devastating and credible analyses of his conduct by human rights groups, who accuse his security forces of systematically killing, kidnapping, imprisoning, and torturing real and presumed political opponents." The upshot, Caryl added, is that the discontented of Uzbekistan will drift "toward the only political alternatives that are radical enough to put up a fight."

Washington excuses its backing of dictators as geopolitical realism, but it sings a different tune when anti-democratic behavior comes from governments that threaten the interests of American corporations. The United States was the only nation in the western hemisphere that did not condemn but welcomed the April 2002 coup that briefly removed Hugo Chávez, the elected president of Venezuela. In fact, Washington funded some of the groups behind Chávez's ouster—incredibly enough, through its National Endowment for Democracy.

There are reasons empires are rarely liked by their subjects, and the United States sometimes seems determined to test each and every one of them. When you boss other countries around, you must expect resentment in return, especially when you refuse to admit, even to yourself, that you boss them. The truth is, the United States—or, more precisely, its government, military, and corporations—infuriates lots of people around the world. Most of them have neither the ability nor the desire to strike back the way bin Laden did, but that doesn't mean they welcome America's domination, or that a few extremists among them won't attempt more forceful action. Improved security against terror attacks is plainly essential, but there is no such thing as a foolproof defense, and revoking the Bill of Rights will not help. After all, America's security agencies possessed plenty of specific information indicating that a terrorist attack was imminent before September 11; the relevant officials simply didn't put two and two together in time. Unfortunately, those officials will probably have a chance to do better next time, because America's own policies seem bound to incite further terrorist attacks.

UPHILL STRUGGLES AND HAPPY ENDINGS

As I was finishing this book, the FedEx man arrived one afternoon with a delivery from New York. The package was heavier than most, and when he learned it was an edited manuscript, he asked what the book was about.

"Why America fascinates and infuriates the rest of the world," I answered.

Without looking up from his clipboard, the FedEx man replied, "Because we're arrogant and rich."

This man was no radical. Olive-skinned, thick around the waist, he was pushing sixty, and he worked hard for his money. His comment stayed with me for two reasons, I think. First, it contradicted the stereotype of the ugly American who revels in the overweening power and wealth of the United States. We have those types, but there are plenty of other Americans who think differently. Second, his answer responded only to the negative half of the American dialectic, the part about infuriating the world; it was as if he didn't hear the part about how we fascinate it. That's a shame. It's important for Americans to remember the myriad virtues and beauties of our nation—not only for accuracy's sake, but because those virtues are what make the nation's faults worth caring about, and trying to correct.

Foreigners sometimes appreciate this dual aspect of the United States better than Americans do, perhaps because they make the crucial distinction between Americans and America. In much of the world, the United States is seen as an arrogant, dangerous bully. But it is also seen as an exciting, inspiring place that combines personal freedom and economic abundance with invigorating energy and inventiveness. While foreigners may occasionally roll their eyes at Americans' naïveté and boorishness, more common is an affectionate admiration for our friendliness, optimism, and unpretentiousness. America is, after all, the world's melting pot. Virtually all the world's nations and races are found here, and it is America's genius to borrow the traditions of the wider world and mix them together into something wholly original that is then shared back with the world.

Now that this book is nearly over, I'm sorry—the inevitable writer's lament—for its shortcomings. I do hope it leaves foreign readers at least somewhat better equipped to live in the Eagle's shadow. But in the end, I'm convinced foreigners can teach Americans at least as much as vice versa, and one place to start is with the lesson that America is more than its foreign policy. Perhaps the greatest lie told to the American people in the aftermath of September 11 is that the terrorist attacks were evidence that "they" hate us. But the world doesn't hate us, the American people. It's our government and military and corporations that irritate foreigners, and often for good reason. If Americans can recognize this distinction, we will better appreciate why our country has a mixed reputation overseas. We will also recognize that "patriotism" is not synonymous with "pro-government," and we will feel more empowered to challenge official American actions that we do not support.

For we Americans cannot escape a certain responsibility for what is done in our name around the world. In a democracy, even one as corrupted as ours, ultimate authority rests with the people. We empower the government with our votes, finance it with our taxes, bolster it with our silent acquiescence. If we are passive in the face of America's official actions overseas, we in effect endorse them.

The first challenge for Americans is to do a better job of informing ourselves about what is going on around the world and our nation's role in it. This won't be easy, because the most readily available information comes from our media, which are greatly compromised by their corporate character and establishment-friendly world view. Our media may as well be a formal part of the government, for all the critical distance they usually maintain. (Which also puts the lie to the common assumption that 75 percent approval ratings in the polls mean that Americans wholeheartedly approve of Bush's approach to the war on terrorism and governance in general. Poll results are only as good as the information they are based on, and the failure of Democrats and the media to offer meaningful criticisms of Bush has left Americans largely ignorant of the alternatives that could be pursued. Just look at how Americans' previous approval of the FBI and CIA collapsed after the agencies' mishandling of September 11–related clues was revealed.) But there are honorable journalists within the corporate media, and if one learns how to read between the lines, much valuable information can be found there. In addition, in the Internet era, alternative outlets, be they political magazines or activist web sites, are only a click away, and so are foreign news organizations, which offer professional-caliber information untainted by devotion to the Washington mind-set.

This book has identified a number of serious problems facing the United States. Our foreign policy is often arrogant and cruel and threatens to "blow back" against us in terrible ways. Our consumerist definition of prosperity is killing us, and perhaps the planet. Our democracy is an embarrassment to the word, a den of entrenched bureaucrats and legal bribery. Our media are a disgrace to the hallowed concept of freedom of the press. Our precious civil liberties are under siege, our economy is dividing us into rich and poor, our signature cultural activities are shopping and watching television. To top it off, our business and political elites are insisting that our model should also be the world's model, through the glories of corporate-led globalization.

Of all these problems, however, the most crippling is our failure to admit that they exist in the first place. How can we fix what we don't know is broken? How can we have an honest discussion about our foreign policy when we don't even admit we are an empire? How can we solve our economic problems when we can't talk intelligently about capitalism or acknowledge that the market can produce bad results as well as good? How can we address any of these problems if we rely on the feel-good fantasies transmitted by our media system, which serve only to distract us from what's important and confuse us about what's true?

So the first order of business, it seems to me, is for Americans to start talking. We'll do ourselves and the world a favor if we turn off the TV, analyze the problems and possibilities confronting us, and begin debating what to do about them. As individuals, we can begin this process today. As a society, we will find it difficult as long as our media and political systems remain dominated by their current governors. How to reform these systems is beyond the scope of this book, but the tools for the job are readily at hand—in the rights guaranteed in our Constitution, in the efforts of the many groups and individuals already addressing these problems, in the inspiring examples found throughout our history of similar social movements that have prevailed.

We need a revolution in America. Not one of violence and disorder, but one of values and ways of thinking, one that remembers where we came from. Our nation was born in revolution. It was dedicated to freedom and fairness, and based on the idea that all citizens could join together as equals to govern themselves. That was a radical idea in 1776, and it remains a radical idea today—and one worth fighting for. No doubt it will be an uphill struggle to reclaim our democracy and fashion it once again into a vessel to be proud of. But I am enough of an American to believe that uphill struggles can have happy endings.

Which brings me to the second volcano. This one was in Hawaii, and I saw it at the very end of my trip, on the way home from Japan. Its name was Mauna Kea, and it was said to be the largest mountain on earth (measuring from the ocean floor rather than from sea level). Unlike Vesuvius, this was a live volcano, and I timed my arrival for dusk, when visibility would be best.

My drive took me through the last tropical rain forest left in the United States. I alternately passed through sun, squalls, and mist, and in the course of half an hour was treated to eight separate, fully articulated rainbows with stunning colors. At the volcano itself, I was lucky to encounter a park ranger who had just set up a long-distance viewscope. Peering through it, I saw, perhaps a mile away, a tongue of red flame shooting out of the mountainside to my left. Seconds later, the ranger alerted me to a second flame emerging from the earth, down at the ocean's edge. Minutes passed, and suddenly the second flame burst into three. A few more minutes and the first flame was joined by two more farther up the ridge, and then another three; the ridge now looked as if it had six different campfires burning.

I absorbed all this in a joyous daze; to see the innards of the earth glowing red before me seemed wonderfully primal. It was dark now, and as I turned to go, I saw a dull orange glow in the sky above the ridge. The ranger said that an entire lake of lava was being reflected in the clouds. Meanwhile, a full moon had risen and was casting a dazzling shimmer across the ocean. By now, even the ranger was impressed. As I walked past, he said, "You're lucky, this is a special night."

And the most astonishing part was yet to come. Driving back through the rain forest, still processing the wonders I had just seen, I thought I saw a rainbow in the distance. But how could that be? It was now perfectly dark. I thought I must be seeing things, or that the wipers had left a smudge across the windshield. But then the road curved, the windshield cleared, and the rainbow was still there, an arc of three gray lines—one light, one dark, one silver—that stretched from one horizon to the other. And there it stayed until I exited the forest five minutes later: my first moon rainbow.

I hadn't known that moon rainbows even existed, and it turns out that they are quite rare. But life is full of surprises, sometimes very pleasant ones. If volcanoes can be beautiful as well as deadly, why can't America be wise as well as powerful, generous as well as rich, magnanimous as well as proud? For all its flaws, this country remains a place where amazing things can happen.

NOTES

As should be evident from the text, much of this book is based on interviews and direct observations made by the author during two extended trips around the world. The more recent trip, conducted specifically for this book, began in May 2001, ended that November, and included stops in Italy, Egypt, South Africa, Zimbabwe, Botswana, Holland, Denmark, Sweden, Germany, France, England, Belgium, the Czech Republic, Spain, and Japan. The earlier trip began in 1991, stretched over six years (including occasional returns to the United States), and featured visits to Holland, France, Italy, Germany, Sweden, Finland, Russia, the Czech Republic, Greece, Hungary, Turkey, Spain, England, Denmark, Kenya, Sudan, Uganda, Thailand, Hong Kong, China, and Brazil. I later visited Cuba and Mexico as well.

In the notes which follow, I do not reference quotes and stories drawn from these travels; I assume the descriptions offered in the text suffice. Rather, these notes offer citations for facts and judgments beyond what I witnessed firsthand. I do not reference every such fact in the text, especially if the text makes clear the source of information; for example, when I quote an editorial from the September 14, 2001, issue of the *Independent* newspaper of London, I do not repeat that citation in these notes. Nor will I burden the notes with references for such widely reported remarks as George W. Bush's statement on September 20, 2001, that foreign nations were either "with us, or you are with the terrorists." I seek simply to indicate the basis for statements that are not self-evident, widely acknowledged, or readily verifiable without special guidance.

NOTES

1. THE PAROCHIAL SUPERPOWER

7 Chirac's comments regarding Kyoto were reported by the Associated Press on March 30, 2001; his criticism of missile defense was reported in the *Houston Chronicle*, June 13, 2001. Blair's and Schröder's concerns about Kyoto were reported in *The Guardian*, March 20, 2001.

10 George W. Bush made three overseas trips on business before he became president—to China, the Middle East, and Gambia, as reported in the *New York Times* of October 29, 2000. Bush's aides later tried to buttress his worldliness by claiming he had made many more overseas trips, but these turned out to be family vacations—to France, Italy, and Bermuda, according to CNN, December 17, 2000.

10 The percentage of Americans with passports was cited by Rudy Maxa, "The Savvy Traveler," found at www.savvytraveler.com, April 13, 2001.

11 The Pew Center's poll was released on December 19, 2001, and is found on the center's web site, www.people-press.org.

15 Bush's 75 percent approval rating was reported in *Time*, March 25, 2002.

16 The businessman's letter appeared in the September 17 issue of *Bild*.

16 Brit Hume's comment was reported in the *New York Times*, December 3, 2001.

16 Walter Isaacson's memo was reported in the *Washington Post*, October 31, 2001.

18 The CIA's unclassified report, "Global Trends 2015," was released in 2000, was covered by the American news media, and is available at www.cia.gov/cia/publications/globaltrends2015.

19 *Because We Are Americans*, edited by Jesse Kornbluth and Jessica Papin, was published as a paperback by Warner Books in November 2001.

22 Steinbeck's quote, from his 1966 book *America and Americans*, was noted in the *Los Angeles Times Book Review*, March 3, 2002.

22 Tocqueville's "self-adoration" quote is found in *Democracy in America*, translated by George Lawrence and edited by J. P. Mayer (New York: HarperPerennial, 1988), volume 1, part 2, chapter 7.

2. GLAMOROUS AND GLUTTONOUS

26 The definitive account of Mao's famine is *Hungry Ghosts: Mao's Secret Famine*, by Jasper Becker (New York: Free Press, 1996).

27 The 46 percent restaurant figure is from the National Restaurant Association's "Frequently Asked Questions," www.restaurant.org.

28 The FAO's calculations were reported in the *Utne Reader*, November–December 2001.

29 Simone de Beauvoir's quote is drawn from her book *America Day by Day*, translated by Carol Cosman (Berkeley: University of California Press, 1999).

29 Santayana's quote is found in *America: The View from Europe*, by J. Martin Evans (San Francisco: San Francisco Book Company, Simon & Schuster, 1976), page 92.

29 Crèvecoeur's quote is from Evans, *America*, page 65.

30 Lerner's statement comes from his book *America as a Civilization* (New York: Henry Holt, 1987), page 39.

30 Hamilton's quote came from *Broken Image: Foreign Critiques of America*, selected and edited by Gerald Emanuel Stearn (New York: Random House, 1972), page 34.

30 Gorky's quote is cited in Evans, *America*, page 184.

30 America's economic strength in 1918 is described in *The Reluctant Superpower: A History of America's Global Economic Reach*, by Richard Holt (New York: Kodansha, 1995), page 11.

31 The story of the destruction of the rail-based mass transit system in the United States is told most fully in "The Great Transportation Conspiracy," by Jonathan Kwitny, in *Harper's Magazine*, February 1981. The role of government subsidy and suburbanization is described in *Earth Odyssey: Around the World in Search of Our Environmental Future*, by Mark Hertsgaard (New York: Broadway Books, 1998), pages 107–8.

35 The information on America's environmental footprint and the need for three extra planets comes from *Stuff: The Secret Life of Everyday Things*, by John C. Ryan and Alan Thein Durning (Seattle: Northwest Environment Watch, 1997), page 67.

36 Data on China's energy and environmental conditions, and the quote from Zhou Dadi, are found and cited in Hertsgaard, *Earth Odyssey*, especially pages 5–6 and 187 and chapter 5.

37 America's entertainment spending is documented in the *Statistical Abstract of the United States, 2001*, published by the United States Census Bureau.

38 Consumption and recycling trends in the United States are documented in "Cutting the Costs of Paper," Worldwatch Institute, December 11, 1999, www.worldwatch.org.

38 The frequency of advertising on American television was documented

in a study by the American Association of Advertising Agencies and reported in *USA Today*, February 15, 2002.

38 The data on children and television are found in *Rich Media, Poor Democracy: Communication Politics in Dubious Times*, by Robert W. McChesney (New York: New Press, 2000), pages 45–47.

39 Bill Bryson's observations are found in *I'm a Stranger Here Myself: Notes on Returning to America After Twenty Years Away* (New York: Broadway Books, 1999), pages 244–46.

40 Linda Wardell is quoted in the *New York Times*, December 21, 2001.

41 The poll by the Center for a New American Dream is available on the group's web site, www.newdream.org.

41 The U.S. surgeon general's warnings were reported by the Associated Press on December 13, 2001.

41 The data on the growth of auto use and its consequences are found and documented in Hertsgaard, *Earth Odyssey*, chapter 3.

42 The *New York Times* story about traffic jams in Los Angeles appeared on March 10, 2002.

43 The Green Deal program is described in more detail in the final chapter of Hertsgaard, *Earth Odyssey*, as well as in a special Earth Day edition of *Time*, Spring 2000.

3. TAKING FREEDOM FOR GRANTED

47 The statements regarding human rights in Russia and the Pasko case were reported in the *New York Times* of January 3 and February 14, 2002, respectively.

50 The provisions of the "USA PATRIOT Act" were analyzed most thoroughly by Ronald Dworkin in *The New York Review of Books*, February 28 and April 25, 2002, and by Nat Hentoff in "Why Should We Care? It's Only the Constitution," in *The Progressive*, December 2001, which also contains the opinion polls.

51 Senator Feingold's remark was reported in Hentoff, "Why Should We Care?"

51 Congressman Kucinich's comments came during a speech he gave on February 17, 2002, in Los Angeles at an event sponsored by the Southern California Americans for Democratic Action.

53 The detention of twelve hundred aliens was reported in the *New York Times*, March 15, 2002.

54 The "truly abysmal" ignorance of America's high school seniors was re-

ported in the *New York Times* on May 10, 2002. The 1995 test was discussed by Lewis H. Lapham in a December 2, 1995, op-ed article for the *Times*.

56 The 3 percent landownership figure is provided in *A People's History of the United States*, by Howard Zinn (New York: HarperCollins, Perennial Classics, 2001), chapter 5, especially page 98.

56 The quote from Adams and Hamilton is found in *American Aurora*, by Richard N. Rosenfeld (New York: St. Martin's Press, 1997), page 3.

57 James W. Loewen's book is *Lies My Teacher Told Me: Everything Your American History Textbook Got Wrong* (New York: New Press, 1995). The story of the lynching photograph and court case is found on page 160.

58 Sheridan's remarks are found in Loewen, *Lies My Teacher Told Me*, page 108.

58 The discussion of the Indian Removal Act of 1830 is based on *What Every American Should Know About American History*, by Alan Axelrod and Charles Phillips (Holbrook, Mass.: Bob Adams, Inc., 1992), pages 107–9.

58 The quote from President Grant's commission is found in *The American Reader: Words That Moved a Nation*, edited by Diane Ravitch (New York: HarperCollins, 1991), page 168.

58 The influence of Iroquois ideas is described in *In the Absence of the Sacred: The Failure of Technology & the Survival of the Indian Nations*, by Jerry Mander (San Francisco: Sierra Club Books, 1991), pages 230–39, which draw heavily on the scholarly work of Donald Grinde, especially his book *The Iroquois and the Founding of the American Nation* (San Francisco: Indian Historian Press, 1977).

59 The "peculiar experience" and "immense irony" quotes are from *Jazz: A History of America's Music*, by Geoffrey C. Ward and Ken Burns (New York: Knopf, 2000), pages vii and 107.

59 The projections regarding American ethnic diversity in 2050 are found in *Chasing the Red, White, and Blue: A Journey in Tocqueville's Footsteps Through Contemporary America*, by David Cohen (New York: Picador, 2001), pages 222–23 and 14, respectively.

60 The National Academy of Science's study was reported in the *New York Times*, March 21, 2002, which also carried a story documenting that black and Hispanic drivers are stopped far more often than whites by New Jersey police.

60 The United States government's actions regarding internees were re-

ported on CNN.com on June 12, 1998, following President Clinton's apology to an additional twenty-two hundred people of Japanese ancestry in South America.

61 George W. Bush's comments about King were reported in the *New York Times*, January 22, 2002.

4. THE OBLIVIOUS EMPIRE

69 Bush's 77 percent approval rating was reported in *Time*, February 4, 2002.

69 The justification for the 350,000 figure, which is considerably lower than some frequently cited estimates, is discussed in "A Hard Look at Iraq Sanctions," by David Cortright, *The Nation*, December 3, 2001.

69 Americans' views of the Middle East conflict were examined in a poll conducted by the Program on International Policy Attitudes of the University of Maryland, released to the media on May 8, 2002, and available via the program's web site at www.pipa.org.

70 Gerald Celente's quote appeared in the *Financial Times* of September 29–30, 2001.

71 Bush's speech was reported, and praised, in the November 11 edition of the *New York Times*.

72 The first Bush administration's grand strategy is described in *The New Yorker* of April 1, 2002.

72 Bush's rejection of the verification protocol for biological weapons was analyzed by Milton Leitenberg in the *Los Angeles Times Book Review*, October 28, 2001.

73 Rupert Cornwell's remark appeared in *The Independent* on July 27, 2001.

76 Dick Cheney was one of only eight members of Congress who voted against the resolution urging the government of South Africa to release Mandela from jail and initiate negotiations with the African National Congress. See Joe Conason's story in Salon.com, August 1, 2000.

77 Kissinger's quote about Chile and his activities with the Forty Committee are described in "The Case Against Henry Kissinger," by Christopher Hitchens, in *Harper's Magazine*, February and March 2001.

77 The death toll resulting from the 1973 coup in Chile is documented by John Dinges in *The Condor Years: How Pinochet and His Allies Brought Terrorism to Three Continents* (New York: New Press, 2003), chapter 1.

78 The findings of the United Nations–sponsored Commission for Historical Clarification, as well as American support for Asian dictators, were

summarized in *Blowback: The Costs and Consequences of American Empire*, by Chalmers Johnson (New York: Henry Holt, Owl Books, 2001), pages 14 and 25–27, respectively.

80 Kwitny's phrase was the title of his illuminating and comprehensive book *Endless Enemies: The Making of an Unfriendly World* (New York: Congdon & Weed, 1984).

81 The quotes from Johnson, *Blowback*, are from pages 33 and 4, respectively.

81 The definitive account of America's actions in Iran, including the help that the local *New York Times* correspondent gave to the coup plotters, is found in Kwitny, *Endless Enemies*, pages 161–78.

82 "The whole Muslim world . . ." quote is from the *Times* of January 31, 2002.

83 American arms sales are described in Johnson, *Blowback*, page 88.

83 The power and role of Trident submarines in America's nuclear arsenal are described by Ramsey Clark, the former attorney general of the United States, in an interview with *Sun* magazine, August 2001.

85 America's role in keeping Toyota from bankruptcy is described in Holt, *The Reluctant Superpower*, page 150.

5. OUR PALACE COURT PRESS

89 Halliday's comments appeared in an interview with Salon.com, March 20, 2002.

89 Rather's quote came during an appearance on *Late Night with David Letterman*, September 17, 2001.

90 Reston's quote appears on page 66 of *On Bended Knee: The Press and the Reagan Presidency*, by Mark Hertsgaard (New York: Farrar, Straus and Giroux, 1988).

91 Liebling's quote is found in the book-length collection of his essays for *The New Yorker* magazine, *The Press* (New York: Pantheon, 1981), page 32.

92 The identity and revenues of the corporations that dominate the American news media were reported in *The Nation*, January 7–14, 2002.

93 Moonves's quote is from *The New Yorker*, December 10, 2001.

93 The 1998 poll reporting the "liberal" views of Washington journalists was cited in McChesney, *Rich Media, Poor Democracy*, page 296.

96 The Ray Bonner story is told in detail in chapter 9 of Hertsgaard, *On Bended Knee*.

NOTES

96 Park's analysis of the obstacles to missile defense came in an interview with the author. For a fuller description of the technical unfeasibility of missile defense, see the various reports compiled by the Union of Concerned Scientists, available on their web site, www.ucsusa.org, as well as Walter C. Uhler's "Missile Shield or Holy Grail?," in *The Nation*, January 28, 2002. The $238 billion price tag for the missile defense system was contained in a Congressional Budget Office study reported in the *New York Times* on February 1, 2002.

100 Reagan's deregulation of television is described in detail in Hertsgaard, *On Bended Knee*, chapter 8.

101 The censorship of journalists at NBC and ABC (and other media companies) is described in McChesney, *Rich Media, Poor Democracy*, pages 52–60.

102 The 1996 Telecommunications Act is analyzed in McChesney, *Rich Media, Poor Democracy*, pages 75–76.

103 Powell made his "angel" quote in an April 1998 speech before the American Bar Association, reported by Mark Crispin Miller in "What's Wrong with This Picture?," in *The Nation*, January 7–14, 2002.

103 The February 19 court ruling was reported in the *New York Times* of February 20, 2002.

105 Simon Marks's article, "Asleep at the Switch: Journalism's Failure to Track Osama bin Laden," appeared in the *The Quill*, December 2001.

107 Doug Struck's comments appeared in the *Washington Post*, February 17, 2002.

107 Kovach and Rosenstiel's article appeared on the op-ed page of the *New York Times*, January 29, 2002.

108 Massing's article appeared in *The Nation*, October 15, 2001.

108 Marc Herold's report can be found at http://pubpages.unh.edu/ ~mwherold.

109 The "Justice Not Vengeance" advertisement and its list of signatories can be found at www.ips-dc.org.

6. AMERICA'S GODS, HOLY AND UNHOLY

116 Rebelle's "food is fuel" quote was reported in the *Utne Reader*, November–December 2001.

117 Freud's quote is cited in Stearn, *Broken Image*, page 214.

119 The increase in Americans' gun purchases after September 11 was reported by Nicholas Kristof in the *New York Times*, March 8, 2002.

120 The Oscar Wilde story is recounted in Stearn, *Broken Image*, page 147.

121 Griffin's quote is from Stearn, *Broken Image*, page 151.

125 The percentages of Americans who hold various religious beliefs are reported in Cohen, *Chasing the Red, White, and Blue*, pages 167 and 202.

127 The Harry Potter challenges were cited by Beverly Becker of the American Library Association; see www.education-world.com.

129 Tocqueville's "Never have I been so conscious . . ." quote and his insights about the relationship between religion and money in America are discussed in Cohen, *Chasing the Red, White, and Blue*, pages 172–77.

130 That thirty-seven thousand forms of faith are practiced in America is documented in *A New Religious America: How a "Christian Country" Has Become the World's Most Religiously Diverse Nation*, by Diana L. Eck (San Francisco: Harper San Francisco, 2001).

7. THE LAND OF OPPORTUNITY TURNS SELFISH

134 Yip Harburg's quote was reported in "E. Y. Harburg and the Wonderful Wizard of Oz," by Francis MacDonell, *Journal of American Culture*, volume 13, number 4, 1990, pages 71–76.

138 The story of Ricardo Morales was reported in the *New York Times* of March 25, 2002.

138 Barbara Ehrenreich's book is *Nickel and Dimed: On (Not) Getting by in America* (New York: Metropolitan Books, 2001).

139 The discussion of stock ownership in America draws on Thomas Frank's brilliant book, *One Market Under God: Extreme Capitalism, Market Populism, and the End of Economic Democracy* (New York: Anchor Books, 2000), especially pages 12 and 96–97, as well as *If the Gods Had Meant Us to Vote They Would Have Given Us Candidates*, by Jim Hightower (New York: HarperCollins, 2001), especially pages 217 and 225.

139 The discussion of income draws on the two books just cited, as well as on Cohen, *Chasing the Red, White, and Blue*, on Doug Henwood's "Spreading the Wealth" in *The Nation* of January 8–15, 2002, and on the Census Bureau's data as found on the web at www.census.gov/hhes/www/income.html.

139 Americans' longer working weeks are documented in *The Overworked American*, by Juliet Schor (New York: Basic Books, 1991).

141 The inflated prices that military contractors charge are documented in "Pick Pocketing the Taxpayer: The Insidious Effects of Acquisition Reform," a report by the Project on Government Oversight, a public

interest group in Washington, D.C.; the report is based on studies by the federal government's General Accounting Office and Pentagon inspector general and was released in March 2002.

142 The data on income shifts come from Cohen, op. cit.

145 The quadrupling of corporate mergers in the United States in the 1980s is reported in Holt, *The Reluctant Superpower*, pages 222–23.

146 The effects of Clinton's earned income tax credit were described by Robert McIntyre of Citizens for Tax Justice, in Washington, D.C., in an interview with the author.

147 The *Business Week* quote is from a story by David Leonhardt, published on March 17, 1997.

147 The hunger statistics were reported in the *San Francisco Chronicle*, November 14, 2001.

148 David Cohen's information about future jobs is found in *Chasing the Red, White, and Blue*, pages 103–4.

150 Litzenberg's quote is from Cohen, *Chasing the Red, White, and Blue*, page 79.

152 Polls showing Americans' support for increased welfare state programs are cited in Hightower, *If the Gods Had Meant Us to Vote They Would Have Given Us Candidates*, page 416, and in *Lost in Washington: Finding the Way Back to Democracy in America*, by Barry M. Casper (Amherst: University of Massachusetts Press, 2000).

8. THE TRAGEDY OF AMERICAN DEMOCRACY

156 The comments from the *Hindustan Times* and *Mail & Guardian* are reprinted in *Jews for Buchanan*, by John Nichols (New York: New Press, 2001), page 24.

158 The discussion of the media's performance draws on Nichols, *Jews for Buchanan*, as well as articles in *Brill's Content* from February 2001, the *Columbia Journalism Review* of January–February 2001, and hearings before the U.S. House Committee on Energy and Commerce on "Election Night 2000 Coverage by the Networks," held on February 14, 2000.

159 Buchanan's quotes are found in Nichols, *Jews for Buchanan*, pages 79–90, especially page 90.

160 Lichtman's comments appeared in an article he published in the *Baltimore Sun* on March 5, 2002.

161 The discussion of the vote list purging and Election Day harassment of

blacks draws on Nichols, *Jews for Buchanan*, pages 27–58, and on Palast's book, *The Best Democracy Money Can Buy* (London: Pluto Press, 2002).

161 The *Pittsburgh Post-Gazette* story appeared on December 2, 2000.

162 The conflicts of interest of Justices Thomas and Scalia are detailed in Nichols, *Jews for Buchanan*, pages 205–9.

162 The *New York Times* story appeared on November 12, 2001.

162 The data on voter turnout come from "Voter Turnout Since 1945— A Global Report," by the International Institute for Democracy and Electoral Assistance in Stockholm; see www.idea.int/vt/survey/voter_turnout2.cfm.

164 The $500 million figure is based on industry estimates and reported in McChesney, *Rich Media, Poor Democracy*, page 263.

165 Bush and Gore's 2000 campaign funding figures are available from the Center for Responsive Politics, www.opensecrets.org.

166 That the richest 4 percent of Americans provide nearly all individual campaign contributions, and that corporations outdistance labor unions by seven to one, are reported in the indispensable book *The Buying of the President 2000*, by Charles Lewis and the Center for Public Integrity (New York: Avon Books, 2000), pages 11 and 28.

166 Pentagon workers' purchases of prostitution and breast enhancement services were revealed in a General Accounting Office report released on July 17, 2002, in hearings before the House Government Efficiency, Financial Management, and Intergovernmental Relations Subcommittee.

168 Among the polls showing public support for including Buchanan and Nader in the 2000 presidential debates was that of James Zogby, released on April 11, 2000.

172 The Gallup poll of 1999 was cited by Jeff Cohen in "Nader Has the Numbers but Buchanan Has the Limelight," *Baltimore Sun*, April 16, 2000.

173 President Bush's appearance before Republican donors in February 2002 was reported by the Associated Press in a story that appeared in the *Baltimore Sun* on February 17, 2002.

173 The positive effects of public finance laws—increased voter turnout, opening the system to nonwealthy candidates, exposing incumbents to meaningful challenges—are described in Hightower, *If the Gods Had Meant Us to Vote They Would Have Given Us Candidates*, pages 190–94.

NOTES

9. LOOK OUT, WORLD, HERE WE COME

180 The ranking of McDonald's and Kentucky Fried Chicken is reported in *Jihad vs. McWorld: Terrorism's Challenge to Democracy*, by Benjamin R. Barber (New York: Ballantine Books, 2001), page 18.

184 The marketing survey and quotes about the "New World Teen" and "a lot of angst" are from *No Logo: Taking Aim at the Brand Bullies*, by Naomi Klein (New York: Picador, 1999), pages 118–20 and 129.

185 The facts from McChesney's book, *Rich Media, Poor Democracy*, are found on pages 79–80 and 86.

185 The facts from Barber's book, *Jihad vs. McWorld*, are from pages 92–93.

186 The corporations that dominate global media industries are described and documented in McChesney, *Rich Media, Poor Democracy*, pages 86–100. The fight over the EU's proposed 50 percent content law is detailed on page 83.

187 The prominence of American TV shows and stars on Egyptian television was attested by interviews with Abdel Monem Said Aly, director of the Al-Ahram Center for Political and Strategic Studies in Cairo, and with other Egyptians, as well as by the author's viewing of Egyptian television.

187 The commercialization of British, Dutch, and Swedish public broadcasting entities and the viewing habits of French children are reported in McChesney, *Rich Media, Poor Democracy*, pages 252–54 and 81, and confirmed in the author's conversations with broadcasting colleagues and other sources in those countries.

190 Umberto Eco's quote appeared in *La Repubblica* on June 7, 2001.

192 The Labour government's plans were reported in the *New York Times* on April 18, 2001.

193 The summary of the critics' case against globalization is based on the author's interviews with Susan George of ATTAC and John Cavanagh and Martin Khor of the International Forum on Globalization, as well as on these groups' position papers, including "Does Globalization Help the Poor?," published by the IFG in August 2001, and "A Better World Is Possible!," published in February 2002, and available through the group's web site, www.ifg.org. See also *The Case Against the Global Economy: And for a Turn Toward the Local*, edited by Jerry Mander and Edward Goldsmith (San Francisco: Sierra Club Books, 1996), and *Global Backlash: Citizen Initiatives for a Just World Economy*, edited by Robin Broad (Lanham, Md.: Rowman & Littlefield, 2002). Khor's

quote about a "double standard" comes from Marc Cooper's article "From Protest to Politics," in *The Nation*, March 11, 2002. The $100 billion price tag of rich countries' protectionism is based on a World Bank study cited in *Time*'s December 31, 2001, issue.

194 The Institute for Policy Studies report can be found on the group's web site, www.ips-dc.org.

195 The Annan and Gates quotes are from the *New York Times*, February 5, 2002. The *Times*'s report on the Monterrey conference appeared on March 23, 2002.

195 The African development plan and ATTAC's and Blair's support for this quasi–Marshall Plan were described in the European editions of *Newsweek*, June 25 and July 30, 2001, and *Time*, August 13, 2001, in the *International Herald Tribune* of August 7, 2001, and in Blair's September 2001 speech to the Labour Party conference, reported in the *Tribune* of October 5, 2001.

10. AMERICA THE BEAUTIFUL

197 Osama bin Laden's quote was reported in the *International Herald Tribune* of September 13, 2001.

199 Rumsfeld made his "ten or fifteen other countries" remark during a press briefing on January 16, 2002, that was broadcast on CNN.

200 The *De Standaard* quote was cited in a February 27, 2002, story by Oliver Libaw on ABCNews.com. Kaletsky's article was published on February 7, 2002.

200 For background on Bush's actions regarding the IPCC, OPCW, and ICC, see the *New York Times* of April 23, 2002, and *The Nation* of April 29, 2002.

201 Rice's comments were reported in *The New Yorker* of April 1, 2002. Donald Rumsfeld also likened the war on terrorism to the Cold War in his press briefing of October 8, 2001.

201 The administration's comments about Americans' supposed new willingness to support overseas wars are found in *The New Yorker* of April 1, 2002.

204 Ambassador Wendt's letter was published on September 17, 2001. His previous postings were confirmed in an interview with the author.

206 Annan's remarks about terrorism and poverty were reported in the *New York Times*, March 7, 2002.

207 Chirac's views were reported in the *New York Times*, March 21, 2002. Peel's article appeared in the *Financial Times* on September 17, 2001.
208 Caryl's article appeared in the *New York Review of Books* on April 11, 2002.
209 American funding of groups behind Chavez's ouster was reported in the *New York Times*, April 25, 2002.

ACKNOWLEDGMENTS

My thanks go first of all to the hundreds of individuals throughout the world whose opinions and curiosity about America inspired me to write this book. Some are named in the text; all are thanked here. I'm also grateful to the authors and journalists whose work I quote, and I urge readers to explore their writing in depth.

I also thank my literary agents, both at home and abroad; I'm especially grateful to Ellen Levine and Diana Finch in New York for representing this book with such passion and skill.

To my editors and publishers around the world: Thank you, colleagues, for believing in this book and sending it forth into the world. I particularly thank Jonathan Galassi in New York and, in Europe, Eva Cossee and Christoph Buchwald for the conversation at their kitchen table in Amsterdam that showed me the way.

Thanks to Michael Lerner and the staff at *Commonweal* for providing me with a quiet and beautiful writing space, and to my colleagues at NPR's "Living on Earth" program for picking up the slack while I was occupied with this book.

ACKNOWLEDGMENTS

Thanks to all my early manuscript readers—Denny May, Mark Cohen, Tom Devine, Mark Schapiro, Francesca Vietor, John Alves, Diana Finch, Ellen Levine, Christoph Buchwald, Jonathan Galassi, Bill Swainson, and the gang at Bloomsbury—for comments that were swift, sure, and illuminating. I also thank Paul Slovak, Nathan Johnson, Mark Dowie, Steve Talbot, David Fenton, Lisa Simeone, David Corn, Steve Cobble, Camilla Nagler, Joan Walsh, Jonathan King, Beth Daley, Paul Robbins, Stephanos Stephanides, Mark Childress, Jane Kay, Eric Brown, Sarah Anderson, John Dinges, and Shoon Murray for advice, information, and support. Finally, special thanks to the always capable James Wilson at Farrar, Straus and Giroux.

My warmest thanks go to my friends and family, and above all to my wife, Francesca Vietor, who stood with me in so many ways throughout this project, and even helped find the title. You're the best.

INDEX

233

INDEX